WRITERS AND THEIR WORK

SAMUEL TAYLOR COLERIDGE

SAMUEL TAYLOR COLERIDGE

from an unfinished portrait of 1806 by WASHINGTON ALLSTON
courtesy of the Fogg Art Museum, Harvard University Art Museums,
on loan from the Washington Allston Trust

SAMUEL TAYLOR COLERIDGE

Stephen Bygrave

NORTHCOTE

BRITISH COUNCIL

ATLANTIC
PUBLISHERS & DISTRIBUTORS (P) LTD

This edition is published by

ATLANTIC

PUBLISHERS & DISTRIBUTORS (P) LTD

7/22, Ansari Road, Darya Ganj, New Delhi-110 002
Tel: 40775252, 23273880, 23275880, 23280451; Fax: +91-11-23285873
E-mail: orders@atlanticbooks.com; Web: www.atlanticbooks.com

By arrangement with
Northcote House Publishers Ltd
Horndon House, Horndon, Tavistock, Devon, PL19 9NQ,
United Kingdom. (T)+44(0)1822 810066; (F)+44(0)1822 810034
(E) northcote.house@virgin.net and (W) www.northcotehouse.co.uk
The *Writers and their Work* series is published in association with
the British Council.

First Indian Reprint 2010
First published in 1997 by Northcote House Publishers Ltd

ISBN 978-81-269-1310-7

British Library Cataloguing-in-Publication Data
A catalogue record for this book is available from the British Library

Typeset by PDQ Typesetting, Newcastle-under-Lyme
Printed in India at Nice Printing Press, A-33/3A, Site-IV,
Industrial Area, Sahibabad, Ghaziabad, U.P.

Contents

Biographical Outline

1772 Samuel Taylor Coleridge born on 21 October at Ottery St Mary in Devon, youngest of ten children of the Revd John and Ann Coleridge (*née* Bowdon).

1781 Kant, *Kritik der reinen Vernunft* (*Critique of Pure Reason*), Schiller, *Die Räuber* (*The Robbers*), published.

Coleridge's father dies.

1782 After six weeks at prep school in Hertford, goes to Christ's Hospital in London as a 'sizar' ('charity boy'), where Charles Lamb is a fellow-pupil.

1789 French Revolution: Fall of the Bastille (14 July); Declaration of the Rights of Man (4 August).

1790 Edmund Burke, *Reflections on the Revolution in France.*

1791 Thomas Paine, *The Rights of Man*, Part I, published.

Deaths of Coleridge's brother Luke and sister Anne (Nancy). Matriculates at Jesus College, Cambridge.

1792 London Corresponding Society and Association for the Preservation of Liberty and Property against Republicans and Levellers formed. French royal family imprisoned. September massacres in France. Continental allies invade France. Thomas Paine, *The Rights of Man*, Part II, published.

Coleridge wins prize for a Greek ode on the slave trade.

1793 France declares war on Britain, which responds on 11 February. Seditious Publications Act limits freedom of the press. Scottish Treason Trials. In France, trial and execution of Louis XVI and the period of the Terror. William Godwin, *Political Justice*, published.

Coleridge attends the trial of William Frend for sedition and defamation of the Church in Cambridge. His first published poem appears in the *Morning Chronicle*. Enlists in 15th Light Dragoons as Silas Tomkyn Comberbache.

1794 Habeas Corpus suspended (until 1801). Treason Trials: Thomas Hardy, Horne Tooke, and John Thelwall acquitted. Paine, *Age of Reason*, Part I, published. Robespierre is executed.

Coleridge meets Robert Southey, and later Thomas Poole. Becomes engaged to Sara Fricker. Involved with Southey and others in Pantisocracy scheme. Leaves Cambridge without graduating.

1795 Directory in France. Suspension of Habeas Corpus renewed in Britain. Treason and Sedition Acts passed.

Coleridge settles in Bristol, where he gives political lectures and meets Wordsworth. Marries Sara Fricker and moves to Clevedon, Somerset. Pantisocracy abandoned.

1796 British peace talks with France fail. Robert Burns dies.

Coleridge launches *The Watchman* (which survives ten issues). *Poems on Various Subjects*, his first book, published. A son, Hartley Coleridge, born.

1797 Failure of French landing in Wales.

Coleridge is at Stowey, then Racedown. William and Dorothy Wordsworth rent Alfoxden House. *Poems, To Which Are Now Added, Poems By Charles Lamb And Charles Lloyd* published.

1798 Habeas Corpus suspended again. Napoleon invades Switzerland (January). Rumours of impending French invasion (April).

Coleridge accepts a position as Unitarian minister of Shrewsbury (where William Hazlitt hears him preach), then withdraws to accept an annuity of £150 from Josiah Wedgwood. Wordsworth and Coleridge, *Lyrical Ballads*, published. A second son, Berkeley, is born. *Fears in Solitude, France: An Ode, Frost at Midnight* published. Sails with William and Dorothy Wordsworth to Hamburg.

1799 Napoleon Bonaparte returns from Egypt, overthrows Directory in *coup* of 18th Brumaire, and is made First Consul.

Coleridge studies at the University of Göttingen, which is where he hears that Berkeley Coleridge has died. Returning to England, he takes his first tour of the Lakes with Wordsworth and meets and falls in love with Sara Hutchinson at the family's farmhouse at Sockburn-on-Tees where Wordsworth is staying.

1800 Mary Robinson dies.

Coleridge is in London writing for the *Morning Post*. Wordsworth, *Lyrical Ballads*, 2nd edn., including Preface, published. Coleridges move to Greta Hall, Keswick, Grasmere. A third son, Derwent, born.

1801 Illness leads Coleridge to begin taking opium heavily. In the autumn he returns to London to write political journalism.

1802 Peace of Amiens marks a brief respite in the Anglo-French war. Bonaparte has himself proclaimed First Consul for life.

Coleridge returns to Greta Hall. 'Dejection: An Ode' is published. A daughter, Sara Coleridge, born.

1803 War resumes.

Poems published. Coleridge takes tour of Scottish Highlands with William and Dorothy Wordsworth.

1804 Pitt the Younger returns as Prime Minister. Bonaparte has himself crowned Emperor Napoleon I (May) and prepares to invade England.

Coleridge sails for Malta, where he is to be Private Secretary to the Governor, Sir Alexander Ball. He visits Sicily.

1805 Coleridge is Acting Public Secretary at Valletta in Malta. In autumn leaves for Sicily, Naples, and Rome.

1806 In June, fleeing the French invasion, Coleridge returns to England. He separates from his wife, living with the Wordsworths and Sara Hutchinson at Coleorton, Leics.

1807 Wordsworth, *Poems, in Two Volumes*, published. Coleridge hears Wordsworth recite the poem much later published as *The Prelude*. Meets Thomas De Quincey.

1808 Coleridge lectures on literature at the Royal Institution for the first time. He moves to Allan Bank, Grasmere, with the Wordsworths and Sara.

1809 *The Friend* appears at roughly weekly intervals until March 1810. Coleridge also begins contributing to the *Courier*.

1810 Coleridge returns to his wife at Greta Hall, Keswick, then in autumn moves to London to lecture and to seek a cure. Quarrels with Wordsworth.

1811 Coleridge settles with John Morgan (a businessman and fellow Christ's Hospitaller he has met in Bristol) and

Charlotte Brent in Hammersmith. His lectures on Shakespeare and Milton are attended by Byron.

1812 Coleridge and Southey, *Omniana,* published. Coleridge lectures on Shakespeare in London.

1813 Coleridge's tragedy *Remorse* reopens Drury Lane in January and runs for twenty nights. In autumn he moves to Bristol and Bath to lecture.

1814 Wordsworth, *The Excursion,* published. Coleridge taken in by Josiah Wade in Bristol for treatment.

1815 Napoleon escapes from Elba: 'the Hundred Days' follow, ending at the Battle of Waterloo in June.

Wordsworth, *Poems,* published. Coleridge dictates *Biographia Literaria* to John Morgan.

1816 *Kubla Khan, Christabel &c* published. Coleridge moves in with the Gillmans at Moreton House, Highgate, for a month (he stays with them eighteen years, until his death). *The Statesman's Manual* published.

1817 *Biographia Literaria* and *Sybilline Leaves* published.

1818 *The Friend* (revised and enlarged in 3 volumes) published. Coleridge gives three courses of lectures on the history of philosophy and on literature (to March 1819).

1819 Coleridge's publisher Rest Fenner goes bankrupt.

1821 Napoleon dies.

Coleridge dictates his *Opus Maximum* to J. H. Green.

1823 Gillmans and Coleridge move to 3 The Grove, Highgate.

1824 Coleridge is elected Fellow of the Royal Society of Literature. Thomas Carlyle visits him at Highgate.

1825 *Aids to Reflection* published.

1827 On Christmas Day Coleridge attends Communion for the first time since 1794.

1829 Catholic Emancipation.

Poetical Works (2nd edn.) and *On the Constitution of the Church and State* published.

1830 Second editions of *Church and State* and *Aids to Reflection* published.

1831 Coleridge attends the first meetings of the British Association.

1834 Third edition of *Poetical Works* published. Coleridge dies on 25 July at Highgate.

Abbreviations and References

References to Coleridge's works are to the relevant volumes in the Bollingen *Collected Works of Samuel Taylor Coleridge*. The edition of Coleridge's poems in the *Collected Coleridge* has not appeared at the time of writing, and the poems are therefore quoted from *The Complete Poems*, edited by William Keach (London: Penguin, 1997).

The following abbreviations are used:

CC *The Collected Works of Samuel Taylor Coleridge*, ed. Kathleen Coburn and Bart Winer (Bollingen, Series LXXV; London: Routledge and Princeton: Princeton University Press, 1969–)

CL *Collected Letters*, ed. Earl Leslie Griggs (6 vols.; Oxford: Clarendon Press, 1956–71)

CN *The Collected Notebooks of Samuel Taylor Coleridge*, ed. Kathleen Coburn (4 double volumes, each with two parts, one of text and one of notes, so far, 1957–)

P. Wordsworth, *The Prelude, 1799, 1805, 1850*, ed. Jonathan Wordsworth, M. H. Abrams, and Stephen Gill (New York: Norton, 1979) (references are to book and line number of the 1805 text)

The following abbreviations are used for the volumes in *The Collected Coleridge*:

AR *Aids to Reflection*, ed. John Beer (1993), *CC*, vol. ix

BL *Biographia Literaria*, ed. James Engell and Walter Jackson Bate (2 vols.; 1983), *CC*, vol. vii

C&S *On the Constitution of the Church and State*, ed. John Colmer (1976), *CC*, vol. x

F.	*The Friend*, ed. Barbara E. Rooke (2 vols.; 1969), *CC*, vol. iv
L.	*The Logic*, ed. J. R. de J. Jackson (1981), *CC*, vol. xiii
L. 1795	*Lectures 1795: On Politics and Religion*, ed. Lewis Patton and Peter Mann (1971), *CC*, vol. i
LS	*Lay Sermons*, ed. R. J. White (1972), *CC*, vol. vi
SW	*Shorter Works and Fragments*, ed. H. J. Jackson and J. R. de J. Jackson (2 vols.; 1995), *CC*, vol. xi
TT	*Table Talk*, ed. Carl Woodring (2 vols.; 1990), *CC*, vol. xiv

Introduction

A 25 year old who had never been to sea writes a pastiche medieval ballad about a sea-voyage. It remains the best known of all the things he wrote. Readers have responded with a mixture of fascination and puzzlement like that of the Wedding Guest ever since *The Ancient Mariner* first appeared as the opening poem of *Lyrical Ballads*, the anonymous volume of which Samuel Taylor Coleridge was joint author with William Wordsworth, in 1798.

By the time *Lyrical Ballads* went into a second edition (in two volumes) in 1800 *The Ancient Mariner* had been moved to the penultimate position in the first volume, the position it occupied in later editions in 1802 and 1805. The second edition of *Lyrical Ballads* identified Wordsworth as the volume's sole author, although its preface mentions Coleridge's five contributions and singles out *The Ancient Mariner*: 'the Poem of my friend has indeed great defects', Wordsworth writes, and goes on to list them. Nearly twenty years after the poem first appeared Coleridge published another different version (adding the Latin epigraph, and the prose gloss in the margins which is neither the first nor last attempt at explanation) in his collected poems, *Sibylline Leaves*. The text usually reprinted is that from his 1834 collected poems. There are then six published versions of a poem which Coleridge continued to revise, sometimes radically, throughout his life. He seems restlessly compelled to revise a poem within which the Mariner is similarly compelled to repeat and retell his story.

For readers of a poem which casts doubt on where the boundaries lie between dream and actuality, death and life, certainty may come only in the simple referential sentences with which the framing narrative of the poem begins and then with which the mariner begins his narration: 'It is an Ancient Mariner' and '"There was a ship"'. The division of the poem into seven parts points up a structure which is dramatic and which seems to ask to be read in ideal or theological terms. Though it could go on indefinitely, there are two climaxes in the Mariner's account: the shooting of the albatross at the end of Part I – a cliff-hanger – and his blessing of the water snakes at the end of Part IV.

The first of these events is presented as dramatic – if the mariner's timing is perfect, that's because the Wedding Guest's timing is that of the comedy straight man:

> 'God save thee, ancient mariner,
> From the fiends that plague thee thus!
> Why lookst thou so?' – With my cross bow
> I shot the Albatross.
>
> (ll. 79–82)

Coleridge famously called Iago in Shakespeare's *Othello* an example of 'motiveless malignity'. The act of shooting the albatross is perhaps an act of motiveless malignity. It is wanton rather than premeditated but brings awful consequences on the Mariner and his shipmates. It was also suggested by Wordsworth.

One of the many problems posed by the later gloss – the first being whether we read it somehow simultaneously with the ballad, as a running commentary, or separately – is that it offers another layer of interpretation. And this interpretation may not be one that either we or the Mariner would be in a position to make, or would want to. Sometimes it does not explain but rather explains away the mysteries of the poem. Here where the ballad just offers 'I shot the albatross', the gloss has 'the ancient mariner inhospitably killeth the pious bird of good omen'. Well, yes it is inhospitable but there has been no sense of its being 'pious' or 'of good omen'. Only the gloss calls it a crime.

The second instance is that moment of redemption when the Mariner is struck by the beauty of the water snakes and blesses them 'unaware'. He finds he can pray and the albatross hung around his neck 'instead of a cross' falls off into the sea. Having previously found the water snakes 'loathsome', now he finds them 'beautiful':

O happy living things! no tongue
Their beauty might declare:
A spring of love gusht from my heart,
And I blessed them unaware.
Sure my kind saint took pity on me
And I blessed them unaware.

The self same moment I could pray;
And from my neck so free
The Albatross fell off, and sank
Like lead into the sea.

(ll. 282–91)

The Mariner ascribes what happens to a tutelary saint. He reads an aesthetic act as an ethical one, and falls to prayer.

There is what might be called a sacramental reading of the poem which follows the Mariner's own reading of its events. He had earlier found his crewmates 'beautiful' (l. 240), but in the blessing of the water snakes there is a shift from an androcentric viewpoint to a transcendental one. The sacramental reading sees the poem as being about crime and punishment followed by redemption of a kind. (One of Coleridge's early unfulfilled projects was for an epic on the origin of evil.) Such a reading sees the poem as a simple cause-and-effect sequence. A more sceptical reading stresses the arbitrariness of the Mariner's action and its punishment – the latter after all depends on a throw of the dice. Nor does the punishment fit the crime: 200 men die, a boy 'doth crazy go', and the Mariner is condemned to wander the earth. On this reading, then, the pious moral can only be seen as ironic and the gloss as an afterthought. The moral is to do with isolation and communion – walking together to the church, praying together – and with loving all God's creatures: the latter can seem like that Victorian hymn, 'All Things Bright and Beautiful'. Famously Coleridge recounted in 1830 that Mrs Barbauld

> told me that the only faults she found with the Ancient Mariner were – that it was improbable, and had no moral. As for the probability – to be sure that might admit some questions – but I told her that in my judgment the chief fault of the poem was that it had too much moral, and that too openly obtruded on the reader. It ought to have had no more moral than the story of the merchant sitting down to eat dates by the side of a well and throwing the shells

> aside, and the Genii starting up and saying he must kill the merchant, because a date shell had put out the eye of the Genii's son. (*TT* i. 272–3)

In Coleridge's analogy the merchant is to be punished not for sin but for carelessness. He retracts not the moral of the poem but its moralizing. The poem is not amoral, but the moral burden of its events 'ought to have' been ambiguous or indirect. Even as it stands, the connection of cause and effect in *The Ancient Mariner* is rather arbitrary. Does the Mariner receive a vision that is benign or diabolic? (For the Pilot's Boy it is certainly the latter.) The sacramental reading sees the poem as an essentially moral narrative or as a myth which is applicable to all sorts of circumstances. I want to offer a parallel case from the next century, a case that the press at the time called 'The Terrible Tale of the Sea'.

In 1884 the 33-ton yacht *Mignonette* was being sailed to Sydney under Captain Thomas Dudley with a crew of three: Edwin Stephens, Ned Brooks, and 17-year-old Richard Parker. On Saturday 5 July, in a gale between the islands of St Helena and Tristan da Cunha, it foundered and went down in ten minutes. The crew put out in an open boat. Their only food consisted of two tins of turnips and they had no fresh water. On about the fifth day they caught a turtle and made its flesh last a week. Parker had drunk seawater, which was believed inevitably to cause madness. On the twentieth day, after eight days without food and six without water, Captain Dudley said a short prayer. He then severed Richard Parker's jugular vein with his penknife. They caught the blood in the ship's chronometer case, drank as much of it as they could before it coagulated, and over the next four days they ate Parker's body. On 29 July they sighted a sail and, having drifted and sailed more than 1,000 miles, the three survivors were eventually rescued by the *Moctezuma* bound for Hamburg and taken back to Falmouth. After disembarking and reporting the loss of the *Mignonette*, they were, to their astonishment, arrested.

This uncanny and macabre story is related by the legal historian Brian Simpson in a book called *Cannibalism and the Common Law*.[1] It is when these events that took place on the high seas are confronted by the machinery of law on dry land that we can see why they may be relevant to the poem. The three sailors were at first released then rearrested. Brooks agreed to appear as a witness for the Crown. Dudley and Stephens were committed to trial in November at Exeter Assizes, held in the castle. The two men were put on trial for transgressing a law they did not know they had broken. There were precedents, including recent ones, for what they had done, but 'the custom of the sea' dictated that they should have drawn lots. Brooks testified that they had not done so but had killed the smallest and weakest among them. Arthur Collins for the two men was thrown back on challenging the jurisdiction of the court. He argued that, while the ship was subject to British law, the open boat in which the four had put out was not. What's the relationship between the law of the sea and the law of the land? The Ancient Mariner's crew enter territory for which there were no precedents: 'We were the first that ever burst | Into that silent sea.' On the 'wide, wide sea' different laws apply: dead men can sail ships, and so on. For the Mariner, ignorance of the law was no excuse; the two defendants claimed that necessity compelled that normal law be suspended. The jury returned a 'special verdict', agreeing to an account of the facts of the case drafted by the judge but referring the question of whether the two men were innocent or guilty of a crime. The assizes were adjourned to the Royal Courts of Justice on the Strand, this time before five judges presided over by the Lord Chief Justice. In proceedings that had become a shambles, there were four lines of defence. First, that when men are reduced to a state of nature the law does not apply because 'Necessity knows no law'. Secondly, extreme circumstances may take away the power of choice, and murder depends on malice aforethought. Thirdly, there was a utilitarian argument: in extreme circumstances you have to do what benefits the majority even if it is at extreme cost to one. The final, least radical defence offered at the trial conceded that killing is wrong and cannot be justified but may be excused on the grounds that the temptation may have been impossible to resist. On Tuesday, 9 December, 1884, Dudley and Stephens were sentenced to death. Their sentences were eventually commuted to six months' imprisonment by the Home Secretary. Simpson's book sees the sailors, like Coleridge's Mariner (who drinks his own blood), as victims persecuted by the arbitrary law. The Lord Chief Justice of England in 1884 was Sir John Duke Coleridge, whose great-uncle was the poet of *The Ancient Mariner*.

The point of this story has been to suggest that the poem is applicable to other cases in which arbitrary transgression confronts a law which it reveals to be arbitrary too. The allegory, in other words, is seen to end with a moral or spiritual meaning which is, as it were, portable and can be transferred to a set of contingent circumstances different from either those which it recounts or those within which it was written. More sceptical readings tend to see in the poem an allegory of particular problems rather than general truths. A reading of the poem as referring to the historical circumstances of its time is, of course, endorsed neither by the Mariner himself nor by the third-person narrator of the poem – and still less by the gloss.

Attempts to make the poem answerable to the times in which it was written have then to rely on circumstantial evidence rather than direct reference. For instance, the 'bloody Sun' under whose aegis its events unfold can be seen to refer to the war. Coleridge conceived and wrote *The Ancient Mariner* at a time when he had apparently retired from his seditious career as public lecturer and sermonizer, and the author of addresses to the people, ephemeral periodicals, pamphlets, and poems. Later he himself called it 'a work of pure imagination' (*TT* i. 149). 'Imagination' is usually read as being opposed to rather than alongside the 'real'; yet four radicals (including Coleridge's friend John Thelwall) had in 1794 been put on trial for their lives charged that they did 'compass. *imagine*, invent, devise or intend death . . . of our sovereign Lord the King'.[2] Imagination then may not be at such a distance from the world of human action as is often supposed.

In the poem the albatross is hung about the Mariner's neck, then Part III opens with 'I saw a something in the Sky'. These sudden shifts from despair to hope can be connected to the volatility of England in 1797 and 1798 as Coleridge was finishing the poem, with rumour and information abounding on a feared French invasion. The French invasion of the independent republic of Switzerland in January 1798 had turned many radicals from their opposition to the war with France. The submarine rumblings which cause the ship to go 'down like lead' and to whirl the Pilot's boat around near the end are in keeping with much of the millenial imagery of the time. The

Mariner's inability to speak – the 'tongue . . . withered at the root' (l. 131) – may refer to the Two Acts (the 'gagging acts') passed by Pitt's government in December 1795. The 'strange power of speech' the Mariner possesses by the end therefore represents a change. That crucial but puzzling event of the blessing of the water snakes recalls some lines from the earlier 'The Destiny of Nations' (ll. 283–8) in which the breeze purifies an ocean poisonous 'with slimy shapes and miscreated life'. In the poem the 'slimy things' no longer 'crawl with legs' but have become things of 'beauty'. Perhaps, as Patrick Keane concludes on the basis of all this evidence, Coleridge here revokes and repudiates (if not quite recanting) his hatred of 'snake-Pitt' and his government. Drama changes things, and whatever else the blessing is, it's a reconciliation to what had previously seemed 'loathsome'.

Among all the attempts to explain the poem it is tempting to see its frame-narrative as framing the subsequent career of its author. In Thomas Love Peacock's Gothic parody *Nightmare Abbey* (1818) Coleridge is satirized as Mr Flosky, a figure like his own mariner, who 'lived in the midst of that visionary world in which nothing is but what is not. He dreamed with his eyes open, and saw ghosts dancing round him at noontide.'[3] After Coleridge's death Carlyle remembered him in *The Life of John Sterling* (1851) as an older man who 'gave you the idea of a life that had been full of sufferings; a life heavy-laden, half-vanquished, still swimming painfully in seas of manifold physical and other bewilderment', someone who is too long diverted from setting sail and is then swiftly lost on 'the high seas' of philosophy and whose 'life had been an abstract thinking and dreaming, idealistic, passed amid the ghosts of defunct bodies and of unborn ones'.[4] Some contemporaries at least then saw Coleridge as his own Ancient Mariner. Others have suggested that the poem anticipates a personal crisis Coleridge underwent on his voyage to Malta in 1804, during which he wrote new lines for the poem.

On board ship the Mariner reaches what I have called a reconciliation, but to some of Coleridge's contemporaries this would have seemed a dignified term for his betrayal of the ideals of the French Revolution. William Hazlitt, anonymously reviewing in *The Examiner* in 1816 Coleridge's *Lay Sermons* (a work he admits only to reading after having written his review), accuses its author of 'having turned – but to no account' politically and of having become reactionarily nostalgic for regimes the European revolutions had swept away.[5] Following Hazlitt, many discussions of Coleridge have tended to see a movement from idealistic young radical to, depending on your point of view, cynical or realistic old Tory who in age defended the same landed hierarchy and feudal tradition he had so vigorously attacked in his youth. This movement is usually said to have occurred from around 1795 to 1802 (when he attacked Napoleon, British isolation, and the Peace of Amiens in articles in the *Morning Post*). The fact that these dates encompass the writing (though not necessarily the publication) of most of his best poetry has led many to see it as dependent on frustration with and then abandonment of the ideals of a 'revolutionary youth'. Coleridge himself claimed that there was no contradiction with his earlier self: as early as 1794 he was denying that he was a democrat, and none of his contemporaries took up his later challenge, in the second number of *The Friend*, 'to shew, in any of my few writings, the least bias to Irreligion, Immorality, or Jacobinism' (*F.* ii. 25). Coleridge certainly attacked Pitt in lectures and in print through the early war years, but he did so because Pitt had instituted a 'terror' parallel to that in France, tyrannically unbalancing the constitution: Coleridge was never against monarchy, for disestablishment of the clergy, or for radical extension of the franchise, never a friend to France; from the start he was closer to Burke than to Tom Paine, Thomas Spence, or his friend John Thelwall. His 'recantation' (the original title of 'France: An Ode') was ironic: France had changed, not him. His own writings, he would claim, demonstrated consistent principles throughout all the contingent events of his writing life and despite the manœuvrings of party politics. In 1795 he wrote in Burkean terms of the need for 'bottoming on Fixed Principles' (*L. 1795*, 33) and there is a similar insistence in the last work published in his lifetime, *On the Constitution of the Church and State.* Whether particular acts and writings are inductive – derived from prior principles – or whether, on the other hand, 'principles' are deduced from particular acts and writings, the point about principles is that they lie in a transcendent realm outside a contingent world which they judge while being no part of it.

We have seen that *The Ancient Mariner* is not just about a sea voyage. Among other things, it is about telling a story. In the poem, the Mariner's uncanny story is told to a Wedding Guest, who is at first unwilling but then 'the Mariner hath his will'. The Mariner chooses his audience. Like many Gothic and sentimental novels, *The Ancient Mariner* puts its first audience into the work. Finally the story will have profound but mysterious effects on its audience, while its teller will be able to do no more than to repeat it and to seek further audiences. We are explicitly told that there is a lesson to be drawn from his narrative. The Wedding Guest 'listens like a three years' child' to what the Mariner says he 'teaches'. The didactic impulse is if anything strengthened by the revisions, especially by the addition of the gloss. But this teaching is an interminable 'agony' which 'returns': for the Mariner, storytelling cannot teach the answer but only repeat the question. The Wedding Guest never gets into the church but hears the Mariner claim the superiority over ritual of community:

> O sweeter than the marriage-feast
> 'Tis sweeter far to me,
> To walk together to the kirk
> With a goodly company! –
>
> (ll. 601–4)

The Mariner is outside the community though his reason for being outside it is known only to him. He has to move on and find another listener. It is the wedding guest who turns away from the door. We can then see the poem not as anticipating the career of Coleridge as an individual – as writer or as biographical subject – but rather as anticipating three kinds of community with which all his work is concerned: audience, education, and Church.

These roughly will be the concerns of the three chapters which follow, each of which corresponds roughly to a stage of Coleridge's writing career. Nearer its other end, Coleridge begins his preface to *Aids to Reflection* (1825) with some solid Augustan contentions: 'An Author has three points to settle: to what sort his Work belongs, for what Description of Readers it is intended, and the specific end or object, which it is to answer'

(*AR* 5). In this instance he envisages a youthful readership. When he comes to answer the question 'WHAT?', he reassures those readers that 'The answer is contained in the Title-page. It belongs to the class of didactic Works' (*AR* 5). That didactism is the subject of the second chapter. The end it turns out is fourfold: religious, moral, rational, and finally mysterious (*AR* 5–9), which summarizes some of the concerns of Chapter 3. That chapter, headed 'Church', is really about the way the 'idea' of an institution tends to be collapsed into what happens to be there at the time. This has led some critics to follow Hazlitt into seeing Coleridge as an apologist for a supine conservatism, though my argument is rather different. The audience is divided primarily by class – different classes requiring different modes of address – and this is the concern of Chapter 1.

1

Audience

In a note made in Malta on Christmas Day 1804 Coleridge calls himself a 'talkative fellow'(*CN* ii. 2372). The table talk of 'the Sage of Highgate' becomes a work in itself, occupying two fat volumes of the Bollingen *Collected Coleridge*. Works such as the *Theory of Life* and *Biographia Literaria* were wholly or mostly dictated rather than written. In later life, then, Coleridge tends to give monologues rather than to engage in conversation and to interact in the margins of books with past writers rather than with a present audience. This at least is the implication of those descriptions of him as his own Mariner referred to in the Introduction.

The Mariner's 'strange power of speech' is a power over an audience of one, and contemporaries saw Coleridge as being like the Mariner in this sense. Caroline Fox recalled an exchange with his former schoolfellow Charles Lamb in which Coleridge asks 'you have heard me preach I think?', and Lamb replies, 'I have never heard you do anything else.'[1] That anecdote is affectionate but, in accounts like those of Carlyle or Peacock quoted in the Introduction, Coleridge has become, like the Mariner, an obsessive talker whose power of speech may be all that perceptibly remains of an earlier literary and political promise. 'All that he has done of moment, he had done twenty years ago,' William Hazlitt wrote in *The Spirit of the Age* (1825), adding 'since then he may be said to have lived on the sound of his own voice'.[2]

In the note quoted at the start of this chapter Coleridge goes on to connect a style of speech to a habit of thought which is inclusive rather than exclusive, Platonic rather than Aristotelian, and derives from an 'affinity' with the things discussed which, 'tho' it perceives the *difference* of things, yet is eternally pursuing the likenesses, or rather that which is common' (*CN* ii. 2372). We saw such a movement in *The Ancient Mariner*. The Mariner's redemption begins from the point at which he recognizes that he is not separate from the rest of animate creation. But an 'affinity' for 'things' is different from an affinity for people. The Mariner's redemption did not allow him to re-enter the community from which his actions had separated him and seemed to be at the cost of the Wedding Guest's membership of a community as well.

The subject of this chapter is Coleridge's relations with an audience. This is an important topic not only because his writing – and his conversation – may be seen as symptomatic of wider changes but also because of his attempts to found an audience – and to find one. For Coleridge the poet is not at the same time a member of an audience, at least not of a popular audience, though he may create one. If the poet was to be, in Wordsworth's famous phrase, 'a man speaking to men', Coleridge was increasingly a man speaking to himself. I want to begin with the period with which we were concerned in the Introduction, which for Hazlitt was the period of Coleridge's greatest achievement.

In the second half of the 1790s Coleridge's so-called 'conversation poems' are addressed directly to friends and family: they include their audiences within themselves. The usual meaning of conversation is dialogue, an exchange between two speakers. More often what we have in these poems is a monologue in the poet's own person. Wordsworth's 'Tintern Abbey', the poem which closes the 1798 *Lyrical Ballads*, is seemingly about solitary experience and individual memory, but it moves near the end to address a second person, his sister, whom we had not realized to be present. Several times in Coleridge's poems of these years there is a turn to another, named person, to a friend who can approve or validate what the speaker claims has happened within the poem. There is such a turn for example in 'The Nightingale' of April 1798 (subtitled 'A Conversational Poem') to both William and Dorothy Wordsworth. So these are 'conversation poems' in the sense that they form part of a published dialogue with his friend and fellow poet. William massively returns the compliment in the poem his widow entitled *The Prelude* but which in his lifetime was always referred to as 'The Poem to Coleridge'. Coleridge continues the public dialogue in his poem 'To William Wordsworth, Composed on the Night after his Recitation of a Poem on the Growth of an Individual Mind', a recitation to an audience which, as well as Coleridge, had included Wordsworth's wife, his sister, and Sara Hutchinson: 'All whom I deepliest love – in one room all', as a line from a January 1807 version of the poem puts it.

We shall pursue the association of speech with the familial and familiar in the next chapter, but Wordsworth's 'Tintern Abbey' is not only a model for his friend's writing. It is also a paradigm for one kind of Romantic poem, beginning in an attempt to compensate for some negative experience or for the absence of some experience but progressively turning the compensation into the experience itself. Speaking of the loss of a direct or immediate contact with the 'forms' of Nature that he thoughtlessly enjoyed as a younger man, Wordsworth consoles himself: 'Other gifts | Have followed. For such loss, I would believe | Abundant recompense' (ll. 87–9). Coleridge's poem 'This Lime-tree Bower my Prison', published in 1800 but a version of which he sent in a letter to Robert Southey from Nether Stowey dated 7 July 1797, is concerned less with connections through time, as in the Wordsworth poem, than with connections across space, but it too is in one way a compensation for loss or a reassurance for absence:

> sometimes
> 'Tis well to be bereft of promis'd good
> That we may lift the soul, and contemplate
> With lively joy the joys we cannot share.
>
> (ll. 64–7)

That 'lively joy' is similar to what Coleridge will call the Imagination. 'This Lime-tree Bower' begins '*here* must I remain'. The location which is insisted upon is dissolved in the poem – there is a movement from imprisonment to liberation through the imagination; from being deprived of society to a claim for identity and community. This claim is the culmination of a process which has certainly not depended on logic and in which the shifts are as abrupt as in *The Ancient Mariner* ('a delight | Comes sudden on my heart').

Perhaps because the process is not a logical or discursive one there is the sense of an audience, or a need for an audience. There is a need at the end of many of these poems of 1797–8 for someone to verify or to validate the experience which the poem claims to have won. The poems end with socialization, with community, or at least with an impulse towards those things. 'This Lime-tree Bower my Prison' deals with the existence of a parallel, other world which becomes imaginatively available, as it does in *The Ancient Mariner*, with the difference that in this poem the community is only temporarily absent: 'They meanwhile' (l. 5). In both, the first readership of the poems is within the poems. Community begins here.

The letter to Southey gives the poem the following context:

> The second day after Wordsworth came to me, dear Sara accidentally emptied a skillet of boiling milk on my foot, which confined me during the whole time of C. Lamb's stay, and still prevents me from all walks longer than a furlong. While Wordsworth, his sister, and Charles Lamb were out one evening, sitting in the arbour of T. Poole's garden, which communicates with mine, I composed these lines, with which I am pleased. (*CL* i. 334)

The published version prunes away any reference to this trivial – indeed comic – context. Of course the dramatic situation still means that the pleasure taken in nature is vicarious: in the exclamation 'a most fantastic sight!' (l. 18), the word 'fantastic' is used literally. The visual detail in the poem is remembered or imagined rather than immediately perceived. For such loss there is abundant recompense because as a result the visual sense is not overpowering – there is a movement from 'to see' to 'to gaze' (ll. 37–43), a process in which the senses do not overpower the mind but in which the mind and senses are, again in Wordworth's term from 'Tintern Abbey', 'interfused'. There is a blurring or withdrawal of immediate responsiveness ('swimming sense'). This ideal visual process is wished onto Charles Lamb, leading to a transcendent expansiveness as Lamb and the others 'emerge | Beneath the wide wide Heaven' (l. 21).

Compensation or consolation is necessary when there is a gap to be crossed. Here the ash tree, flinging its trunk 'arching like a bridge' across the dell (ll. 12–13), and the rook, which will be seen by separated friends who cannot see each other, each close a gap in the poem. There is a kind of triangle formed between the poet, his friends, and the rook. We might see each point of this triangle as representing an alternative: respectively a solitary and earthbound self, a little community which is absent, and a theologized nature.

We have seen that the poems of these years often culminate in a blessing of some other person, a friend or relative, someone already *known*, who can validate or verify a claim which could not be logically verified or validated. There are two such blessings in 'This Lime-tree Bower my Prison'. In the first (ll. 32–7, which had been written much earlier than the rest of the published poem) the poet wishes on Nature an intensification of its own energy. In the second (ll. 68–73) he blesses a rook. When the Ancient Mariner blessed water snakes, it made possible his return to a community even if he couldn't be assimilated by it. There is a similar moment of inclusion here:

> A delight
> Comes sudden on my heart, and I am glad
> As I myself were there.
>
> (ll. 42–4)

As in *The Ancient Mariner*, this is a climax from which it is necessary to retreat, to bring this visionary claim back into society. In *The Ancient Mariner* there is a return to the known and ordered world of the opening. Things are different in the opening here. The immobilized speaker sees himself as in 'prison'. The metaphor is charged with particular force at a time when the government was indeed threatening its opponents with prison. Though this is only glanced at in a clause, it is a reminder that the dialogue of the poem is not only with an absent guest but with a dangerous world. Years later Coleridge recalled a conversation in the same arbour with the Coleridges' very next guest at the cottage in Nether Stowey, John Thelwall: 'I said to him – "Citizen John! this is a fine place to talk treason in!" "Nay! Citizen Samuel!" replied he, "it is a place to make a man forget that there is any necessity for treason" (*TT* i. 180–1). (Wordsworth's recollection of the conversation in a note to his own poem 'Anecdote for Fathers' is slightly different.[3]) Thelwall's response implies that poetry may be a mode of forgetting rather than transforming the political world. The poem, on the other hand, suggests that its little community may harmonize the dissonances issuing from the state within itself.

The idealized community may at this stage represent an alternative to the British state, even a challenge to it, rather than a consolation for its inevitable dominance.

The domestic poems written in the late 1790s often replay the dialectic of engagement in and withdrawal from public events, in the dialogue between speculative husband and piously reproving wife in their cottage in 'The Eolian Harp', or that rural bower – a good place to reconcile oneself to the world or to escape it all together – in the poem we have just been looking at. It would be possible to see in these poems a concealed version of Coleridge's own gender anxieties and unhappy marriage. In *The Ancient Mariner* the moon is female but so is Death's partner, identified in the version of 1817 as 'the Nightmare Life-in-Death'. There are also certainly anxieties focused on Wordsworth, the latter always seemingly more confident of imposing himself on language and on the world. Coleridge is always unsure of the validity of what has been won in the poem. *The Ancient Mariner* demonstrated how tenuous and provisional the community can be. In 'Tintern Abbey' Wordsworth looks at his sister but sees only himself; he writes in *The Prelude* of how, disappointed at the outcome of events in France, he sought refuge 'in the place | The holiest that I knew of – mine own soul' (*P.* x. 379–80). Coleridge has no such refuge, only metaphysics, opium, and unrequited love for Wordsworth's sister-in-law. He looks to others as much for reassurance and consolation as for echoing confirmation.

If there is an ideal of domestic retirement, then it is an ideal which is to be interrupted. The wedding is celebrated without the Wedding Guest, just as Wordsworth stands apart 'like an uninvited guest' from the prayers of praise offered for British naval victories over the French (*P.* x. 270–4). The audience written into the poems must of course be ideal rather than actual because even intimate friends are not there allowed to speak for themselves – Lamb humorously protested against being called 'gentle-hearted' – and the community must remain an imagined one. In the mid-1790s Coleridge with his brother-in-law Robert Southey and others planned to found a utopian colony on the banks of the Susquehanna River in Pennsylvania. The scheme eventually collapsed, but we might see the poems of the second half of the 1790s as a way of transplanting the ideals of that

'Pantisocracy' project into the aesthetic realm.

Coleridge's sonnet 'Pantisocracy', once attributed to Southey, imagines a 'cottag'd dell' in the new world

> Where Virtue calm with careless step may stray,
> And dancing to the moonlight Roundelay,
> The wizard Passions weave an holy Spell.
>
> (ll. 6–8)

Perhaps these lines anticipate the injunction in the more famous and much less evidently political 'Kubla Khan' to 'Weave a circle round him thrice' – a line itself quoted from the witches in *Macbeth*. As the famous vision of his poem appears to recede, Coleridge summarizes:

> The shadow of the dome of pleasure
> Floated midway on the waves;
> Where was heard the mingled measure
> From the fountain and the caves.
> It was a miracle of rare device,
> A sunny pleasure-dome with caves of ice!
>
> (ll. 31–6)

That word 'midway' is important. It is a word that recurs in several other poems from 1796–9. The *Oxford English Dictionary* calls its use as a preposition 'rare' and dates it from about 1798. To be 'midway' is to be neither here nor there, to be, like the soldiers of the Grand Old Duke of York, only halfway up, neither up nor down. However, as in these lines from 'Kubla Khan', there may be advantages to such an indeterminate state.

The 'shadow' of the pleasure-dome, 'midway' between the perceiver and something else, is not allowed to dominate the perceiving mind but can be mediated by it. We saw such an ideal of perception to be already implicit in 'This Lime-tree Bower'; later, under the influence of Kant, Coleridge works out its implications in some detail. The ideal of perception becomes also an ideal of representation. For instance, 'Extremes meet' becomes a favourite axiom in his notebooks. As we shall see, he is compelled to find the common ground there may be between seemingly irreconcilable positions: to stress, as he puts it, that distinction is not division (*BL* ii. 7). I suggest in this book that Coleridge belongs to or can be recuperated for an English Liberal tradition and the word 'midway' in these early poems may already stand for the *via media* he always seeks.

In 1796 Coleridge published a poem addressed to Lamb, 'To a Friend who had declared his intention of writing no more poetry', in a Bristol newspaper for a subscription for the family of Robert Burns, who had recently died indigent. Burns earns his place on Helicon, the mountain of the muses, not only for his poetry but also because of his closeness to a harsh nature and his tendency to bite the aristocratic hand that fed him. The poem concludes with an appeal to the example of Burns:

On a bleak rock, midway the Aonian mount,
There stands a lone and melancholy tree,
Whose agèd branches to the midnight blast
Make solemn music: pluck its darkest bough,
Ere yet the unwholesome night-dew be exhaled,
And weeping wreath it round thy Poet's tomb.
Then in the outskirts, where pollutions grow,
Pick the rank henbane and the dusky flowers
Of night-shade, or its red and tempting fruit,
These with stopped nostril and glove-guarded hand
Knit in nice intertexture, so to twine,
The illustrious brow of Scotch Nobility!

(ll. 26–37)

The poisoned wreath with which the devotee of Burns is to deck aristocratic brows makes of this poem a challenge to Lamb the lapsed poet but continuing radical sympathizer. The tree which is the working-class poet's instrument grows 'midway' the mountain of the muses. 'France: An Ode', composed in the immediate aftermath of the French invasion of Switzerland in 1798, begins with an invocation of natural objects as entities which are 'free' to 'bear witness ... With what deep worship I have still adored | The spirit of divinest Liberty'. So

Ye Woods! that listen to the night-birds singing,
Midway the smooth and perilous slope reclined,
Save when your own imperious branches swinging,
Have made a solemn music of the wind!

(ll. 5–8)

Coleridge's poem 'Love', published in 1799 and revised for the 1800 *Lyrical Ballads,* is like *The Ancient Mariner* a pastiche medieval ballad with a frame-narrative. In it the narrator wins over his Genevieve by singing her 'an old and moving story' and gets to go to his own wedding. Built in to the frame is a reminiscence of time with the beloved:

> Oft in my waking dreams do I
> Live o'er again that happy hour,
> When midway on the mount I lay,
> Beside the ruined tower.
>
> (ll. 5–8)

We shall see in the next chapter that Coleridge compares the imagination to a ruined tower and these lines offer a positive version of the midway state as one which can be returned to in imagination or in memory. However, the word often functions within a trope of Coleridge's admired Francis Bacon in which knowledge is allegorized as a steep and winding path to be achieved only with much difficulty and digression. Coleridge employs the trope – though not the word – in a poem published in 1797, 'To a Young Friend on his Proposing to Domesticate with the Author'. In 'The Eolian Harp' it is while 'on the midway slope' of a hill that the fond and pious husband is invaded by 'many idle flitting phantasies'. 'Midway' is also the opening word of a poem addressed to Coleridge by Anna Laetitia Barbauld, the Bluestocking poet, essayist, and writer for children, who was mentioned in the Introduction.

> Midway the hill of science, after steep
> And rugged paths that tire the unpractised feet,
> A grove extends, in tangled mazes wrought,
> And filled with strange enchantment ...[4]

Barbauld's poem addresses Coleridge as an equal, offering him advice. He figures as the patient to Barbauld's doctor or, as the last line has it, as a child to a parent: 'Now heaven conduct thee with a parent's love!' The poem does not admonish Coleridge to abandon metaphysics for poetry but warns him not to become lost in it, or not to become stalled by it. The hill is a wooded place in which truth is concealed, or appears as its opposite. It should be a place of rest and not a final destination. 'Science' (German *Wissenschaft*) is only 'midway' to a transcendent truth: it is incompatible with 'the muse'. The temptations of the former are figured as enchantment by a female (Circe, who turned Ulysses' sailors into swine). Narcosis and sexuality are here metaphors for physical and psychological malaise – simply, inactivity. Circe can be 'enjoyed, but still subservient'.

The poem is like a medieval or Renaissance allegory; the narcotic bowers of Spenser's *Faerie Queene* are its model. Barbauld had already used the trope from Bacon in an essay, 'The Hill of Science: A Vision', published in 1773. Her poem was published in 1799, after Coleridge's return from Germany, but was probably written earlier, following Coleridge's visit to Barbauld in August 1797 (*CL* i. 341 n.). The view of Coleridge here – brilliant but sick, short-changing his genius – becomes familiar in his lifetime, as we have seen.

Coleridge's poem 'A Stranger Minstrel', addressed to another female poet, Mary Robinson, was first published in a section of memorial verses appended to Robinson's *Memoirs* in 1801. In an opening sentence of twenty-two lines the poet, lying 'supine | - Midway th'ascent' of Mount Skiddaw, swears by a mountain landscape which recalls the landscape of 'Kubla Khan':

> ... by thy many-colour'd chasms deep,
> And by their shadows that for ever sleep,
> By yon small flaky mists that love to creep
> Along the edges of those spots of light,
> Those sunny islands on thy smooth green height ...
>
> (ll. 13-17)

He recognizes that Robinson's 'soft blue eye was made for' the mountain, which then replies. There is a kind of mock-sublimity in this. The mountain's 'voice was like a monarch wooing' (l. 45), a little joke that would not have been lost on readers who would have known that, before becoming (unusually for a woman) a professional writer, Robinson had been an actress notorious as the mistress of the Prince of Wales.

The recurrence of the unusual word 'midway' in all these instances suggests that the need for visions to be mediated (and perhaps approved) from the outside cannot always be answered by an appeal to an already known community such as that made up by friends and family. Representations, even when unpublished, have a public status that demands a more objective or consensual kind of validation. There is nothing novel about Coleridge addressing friends and family in verse. The novelty arises from his sharp awareness of a gap between private speculation and its public contexts, a gap 'midway' intimacy and publication. This is a gap too wide to be bridged by poetry alone but, rather than abandoning poetry, Coleridge attempts to found a unifying moral and political discourse on the model of his poetics. That poetics in turn is founded on an intimate or familial model.

We saw that there was hope as well as just pathos in the impulse towards finding or creating a community. Such a hope is evident even in the act of solitary reading Coleridge describes in two notebook entries made on board ship bound for Malta in 1804. He notes that in reading epics there is a need for sympathy, for what he calls, quoting his own phrase from 'Frost at Midnight', a 'believing Mind', a patient suspension of the desire for propositional summary and for criticism. This psychological suspension might stylistically be prolixity: 'Does not this dread of Prolixity in ourselves, & criticism of it in others, tend to make all knowledge superficial as well as desultory – incompatible with the pleasure derived from seeing things as they are, as far as the nature of Language permits it to be exhibited' (*CN* ii. 2075). Coleridge's terms here suggest the more famous later formulation from *Biographia Literaria,* his 'literary life' published in 1817, of 'that willing suspension of disbelief which constitutes poetic faith' (*BL* ii. 6), and also a passage from Milton's *Paradise Lost* that Coleridge quotes more than once in print. In the fifth book of Milton's epic the angel Raphael outlines to Adam a process in which all living things from 'body up to spirit work', a process in which they find their being in 'Reason'. 'Things as they are' in the note above are not the things of the material or sensory world; the real is approached in language, through a suspension of attention to what is sensory or material. Such a suspension is not something to be achieved hastily. Impatience or lack of sympathy with 'prolixity' is therefore not only an aesthetic habit, but a philosophical and, as we shall see, a political choice.

The notion that poetry is the expression of the poet rather than the imitation of something which lies outside in the world has become a commonplace of Romantic aesthetics. In the second of these notes of 1804 the objectification or expression of the writer becomes a dream shared with the reader:

> Poetry a rationalized dream dealing to manifold Forms our own

> Feelings, that never perhaps were attached by us consciously to our own personal Selves. – What is the Lear, the Othello, but a divine Dream/all Shakespere and nothing Shakespere. – O there are Truths below the Surface in the subject of Sympathy, & how we *become* that which we understandedly behold & hear, having how much God perhaps only knows, created part even of the Form. – good night – (*CN* ii. 2086)

It is the deification of Shakespeare which is at first most apparent in this speculation. The 'dealing' out of roles in drama is clearly important to it as well. Dissolution of the conscious self is also posited as a collective effect upon an audience who 'behold and hear' rather than on the solitary reader of poetry. In the last full clause it may also be that the audience is credited with the unconscious creation of the form it sympathetically beholds.

A few years later, in a notebook entry of May 1810, Coleridge essays several definitions of poetry, one of which – the balance of local or immediate pleasure with the pleasure to be derived from the poem as an organic whole – he later uses in the *Biographia Literaria* (*BL* ii. 13). The last of these definitions is careful to stifle the implication that a formulaic or enumerative criterion might be possible for the pleasure to be derived from poetry. The poem is to be seen not only as organic but as relatively autonomous:

> Not the mere quantity of pleasure received can be any criterion, for that is endlessly dependent on accidents of the Subject receiving it, his age, sensibility, moral habits, &c – but the worth, the permanence, and comparative Independence of the Sources, from which the Pleasure has been derived. (*CN* iii. 3827)

Here Coleridge is trying to arrive at a definition of the 'permanent' worth of the poem, which for him is to be found not in the relativity of its readings but in the work itself as something which produces an absolute 'pleasure'. The desire for summative and absolute laws is characteristic of Coleridge's later writings, as we shall see, but here it is the way he downplays the contingency not only of the poem's 'sources' but of its subsequent reception that is significant. The 'pleasure' of the poem is to be found within the poem and not in the 'accidents' of its reading.

This chapter began, as the next will, with poems Coleridge wrote in the second half of the 1790s, which for a younger contemporary like William Hazlitt was the period of Coleridge's greatest achievement and also the last time he could still be described as a 'Jacobin'. In the Introduction we noticed Hazlitt's charge that Coleridge was an apostate, reneging on the social and political principles of the 1790s with which Hazlitt himself had kept faith. At the beginning of this chapter I quoted Hazlitt ten years later, in 1825, sounding almost elegiac for Coleridge: 'All that he has done of moment, he had done twenty years ago.' In fact nearly twenty years do separate the planning and publication of *Lyrical Ballads* from Coleridge's critique of those poems and the principles on which they were based in the second volume of *Biographia Literaria.* These chapters from the *Biographia* are largely responsible for the durable influence Coleridge has had upon literary criticism. In them Coleridge consciously repudiates Wordsworth's 1800 'Preface', which he had himself claimed as 'half the child of my own brain' .

The 'Preface' gained a radical, even revolutionary reputation from the social and political implications of its claims for 'low and rustic' speech. In Wordsworth's contestation of the received idea of poetic language as a refined, perfected mode of eloquence available only to those educated in previous literary models Hazlitt found a 'levelling tendency', suggesting implications wider than the extension of the literary franchise in Wordsworth's argument about the language of poetry. By 1817 the 'unfortunately...equivocal expression' Coleridge (mis)-quotes Wordsworth using is 'the language of *real* life' (*BL* ii. 8), and for him the adjective 'real' has a classical sense. He argues that the language of rural life is appropriate for certain kinds of poem, not for poetry, and carefully rejects the inference that 'passion' and 'nature' are inevitably the product of its use. The fundamental elements of language are not be found among a specific class of language-users but rather in grammar, an apparently classless set of principles or rules.

To this extent, Coleridge's classical conception of language fits with a present-day understanding of language as an entity available to but not possessed by any speaker. For Coleridge the truest form of language is that which is the freest from the temporary attitudes and presuppositions of the social world and the best language for poetry is that which is the most universal. Such a language, he goes on, will inevitably be the property of those classes for whom a daily occurrence is the exercise of philosophical and spiritual meditation, rather than physical labour. A particular and disconnected mode of speech is opposed to an educated language which is general and, tending to discover a law in things, moves by stages from grammar to logic. To Wordsworth's imperative that the poet strip away the linguistic and other habits of civilized life among the upper classes Coleridge retorts that, on the contrary, only a socially privileged life provided 'a certain vantage-ground' (*BL* ii. 44), the opportunity for meditation by which general laws and their appropriate language could be attained. The unsophisticated speakers of the rural poor are replaced in the same relation to language as before Wordsworth had written.

This critique of Wordsworth in the second volume of *Biographia Literaria* is part of an attempt to provide a philosophically rigorous defence of poetry. The movement from 'pleasure' to 'truth' Coleridge describes in the reading of a poem is also a movement from the poem to the poet (*BL* ii. 12). The definition of the 'creative imagination' which closes the first volume ought to function as a link to the second. However, instead of using it to introduce his critique of Wordsworth, Coleridge ends chapter fourteen of the *Biographia Literaria* by describing the ideal poet: a figure who brings 'the whole soul of man into activity', in some way giving it substance rather than representing it, not simply imitating a pre-existing phenomenon but giving it birth (*BL* ii. 15–18).

So similarities do remain with Wordsworth's theory of poetic language. For example, Coleridge seems to agree that the poet is distinguished from and, linguistically speaking, superior to the 'low and rustic' protagonists of the *Lyrical Ballads*. The poet is licensed to speak for a community by virtue of being a poet and not by virtue of being a member of that community. Imagination could become a social force only by descent from the individuals who exemplify it, and those individuals are rare. The poet is distinct from the subjects who people his poems just as he is distinct from their audience. The function of the political lectures of the 1790s was 'to disseminate Truth' (*CL* i. 152), that of the clerisy twenty years later to 'diffuse' it. In both cases a route proceeds from the individual privileged to recognize truth to a people in need of receiving it. The former 'should plead *for* the Oppressed, not *to* them' as Coleridge writes in the Introductory address to *Conciones ad Populum* (*L. 1795*, 43). The lecturer's aim in addressing the poor is to illuminate them that revolutionary change may be possible; so they should be taught their duties before their rights. One kind of revolution may then be forestalled in order to seed what is primarily a general moral change.

In 'This Lime-tree Bower my Prison' there was a movement from enforced solitude towards an ideal community. That movement was apparent from the poem as a whole as well as from the local instances of gaps being bridged. This chapter began, though, with another version of the solitary Coleridge, as the ageing monologuist of contemporary accounts, unable to temper his obsessions to an audience who now had their own expectations. That change can be seen as a symptom of two related developments in Coleridge's lifetime: the coming into existence of a mass reading audience served by a proliferation of new publications and the replacement of a system of authorial patronage by a commercial system.

As a result of these changes some who would previously not have done so gained access to publishing and to the social benefits associated with it. However, both trends meant that authors found themselves serving an impersonal market. Authors no longer addressed a patron known to them whom they had to please but rather an anonymous mass readership. Writers of Coleridge's generation and later were offered the possibility of reaching large numbers of readers. Poets such as Walter Scott and Lord Byron became commercially successful in a way previously impossible. The audience was now large – as a 'misgrowth of our luxuriant activity, we have now a READING PUBLIC' (*LS* 36) – and that audience was also unknown and no longer homogeneous. If the market system offered authors of the period hope of influence over large numbers of readers, it also tended to reverse the relative power of reader and audience. A reading audience had its own demands and had an increasing say in the form and content of reading matter that could now be conceived of as commodity, as was the case with Scott and Byron. If the phrase 'Coleridge's audience' is not quite an oxymoron, then the newly meaningful phrase 'a *popular* audience' was mostly beyond him.

Jon Klancher has pointed out that Coleridge could still envisage the audience for his own writing as comprising individuals known to him, as he envisages it in the early poems. Coleridge writes that the successful first night of his tragedy *Remorse* 'did not give me as great or as heart-felt a pleasure, as the observation that the pit and boxes were crowded with faces familiar to me, though of individuals whose names I did not know, and of whom I knew nothing, but that they had attended one or other of my courses of lectures' (*BL* i. 221). However, the *Biographia Literaria* also gives the quixotic narrative of his tours of Bristol and the Midlands to drum up subscribers for *The Watchman*. That periodical failed after a few issues, as *The Friend* was to do later. The readers were not there to be found, but had to be made, not only for the sake of Coleridge as a professional writer but for the health of a society now almost co-extensive with its reading public. For Coleridge, literary production that adapted itself to the tastes and capacities of a mass readership would inevitably be debased: so books of popular science were a 'plebification' of knowledge (*F.* i. 447; *C&S* 69).

The alternative to 'plebification' is to set up institutions which would secure against the influence of the public the wisdom of the few who in any country at any time enjoy privileged access to truth and reason – Coleridge writes in *The Friend*, for instance, that world history is full of 'accounts of noble structures raised by the wisdom of the few, and gradually undermined by the ignorance and profligacy of the many' (*F.* i. 62). Another note made in Malta, in January 1805, begins by observing that an 'execrably educated' British army is now inferior in mathematical knowledge and technical knowhow to the French. This is because the French, despite their private venality, have put their education system on a public, national basis, which leads Coleridge to an imperative: 'the necessity of supporting *Science*, & perhaps every thing, by Government & Patronage.' ('Patronage' here clearly refers to state funding of teaching and research rather than an *ad hoc* or 'jobbing' reliance on aristocratic support.) This is no egalitarian ideal but a means of ensuring that the knowledge of 'the few' is most widely influential. There is otherwise a danger that influence once held by the court, which was bad, will pass by default to the public, which would be worse:

> and now combat stoutly the opinion of a PUBLIC as a good thing/it is Perdition/trace it in every country – while a Court is the great Judge, Poetry & Oratory becomes over-decorous, over delicate, stupid stately/but when men of Learning write to men of Learning, & the number of Readers is small, then rise the Suns, Moons, and Stars out of the Chaos – but when the PUBLIC are the Judge, O Heavens! (*CN* ii. 2395)

What you get then – on the other side of this exclamation – is the 'sickly and stupid' drama attacked in the *Lyrical Ballads* preface with now the omnipresent danger of 'Jacobinism'. If 'plebification' inevitably fostered a kind of reading which participated in commercial society rather than standing reflectively outside it, then education would be crucial in counteracting it. In the next chapter we shall see that Coleridge eventually recommends that, although literary texts will be given no special privileges, education should be based on the interpretation of texts and recommends that the state endow 'the few' who are to educate the many as an autonomous class.

2

Education

The audiences put into Coleridge's early poems are often friends and family, as we have seen. The angle of address to the audiences for later works is often educative – as is suggested by the subtitles of many of them: *The Friend; a series of essays in three volumes; to aid in the formation of fixed principles in politics, morals and religion, with literary amusements interspersed,* or *Aids to Reflection in the formation of a manly character on the several grounds of prudence, morality and religion.* These speak for a pedagogic rather than a didactic concern, an ideal pedagogy which in the 1790s was to be shared with Wordsworth: 'what we have loved | Others will love, and we will teach them how', as the latter writes (*P.* XIII. 444–5). Criticizing Wordsworth in 1817 with the assertion that rural life and labour are not sufficient in themselves, Coleridge writes that 'Education, or original sensibility, or both, must pre-exist if the changes, forms, and incidents of nature are to prove a sufficient stimulant' (*BL* ii. 45). In 'Frost at Midnight', another of the 'conversation poems'of the 1790s, the deficiencies of the poet's education, as he remembers it, are to be remedied by the child's future.

The poem begins in a setting in which all is quiet potential. It rises to a climax in which 'abstruser musings' and the initial setting they apparently suited are enlivened by natural transformation. We as readers are the audience for what it is insisted is not conversation but are rather silent and solitary musings; then in the second half of the poem a similarly dynamic transformation of the speaker's child is promised, enrolling him in a new community. It is not that the speaker is unaware of this energy – a natural 'secret ministry' is insisted on at the start – but that he moves from observer to participant and beneficiary. Initially all the activity of nature is 'inaudible as dreams', though a nature which is immanent and apparently inactive still takes priority over the community: 'Sea, hill and wood | This populous village!'

The film which flutters and flickers on the grate of a low fire becomes an emblem at first of an idle and egotistical spirit and then of a dreamed of community. Coleridge's footnote explains that the 'stranger', as this phenomenon is called, in popular tradition 'portends the arrival of some absent friend'. So strangeness becomes familiarity. The community will comprise not the inhabitants of the 'populous village' but the speaker's child, who is a version of the speaker himself; by implication it includes the reader of the poem too. This community comes to be part of the natural setting rather than merely its tenants.

Once again, though, the speaker is a beneficiary at one remove. He turns to address his – sleeping – child as one who is similar to and different from himself:

> thou shalt learn far other lore,
> And in far other scenes! For I was reared
> In the great city, pent 'mid cloisters dim,
> And saw nought lovely but the sky and stars.
> But *thou*, my babe! shalt wander like a breeze
> By lakes and sandy shores, beneath the crags
> Of ancient mountain, and beneath the clouds,
> Which image in their bulk both lakes and shores
> And mountain crags: so shalt thou see and hear
> The lovely shapes and sounds intelligible
> Of that eternal language, which thy God
> Utters, who from eternity doth teach
> Himself in all, and all things in himself.
> Great universal Teacher! he shall mould
> Thy spirit, and by giving make it ask.
>
> (ll. 50–64)

'The child is father of the man', as Wordsworth wrote in a famous fragment a few years later, and in these lines the child becomes the teacher of the parent. The child here is the vehicle for transformation: the transformation of silence or 'inarticulate sounds' into language and of solitude into community. The child's 'breathings' move from a background rhythm to an animating 'breeze'. In this process education is not finite, but a reciprocal gift.

The poet wishes on the child an ideal which will surpass his own childhood of a 'nature' which is coherent and intelligible as the language of God. This ideal of nature as the signature of an immanent divinity is an ancient one. The child is asleep and cannot answer back, but this is only a more explicit version of the infantilism (Latin *infans*, 'unable to speak' as well as 'child') of the friends and family addressed in Wordsworth's 'Tintern Abbey' or in Coleridge's other 'conversation poems'. The distinction proposed between the speaker and the one spoken for ('for I...but thou') is of course a temporal distinction between the child and the adult, but this empirical distinction is succeeded by a discourse in which the 'therefore' introducing the final paragraph of the poem effaces the differences of the seasons under the universality of logic. Seasonal change cannot affect the constancy of the relationship. The word 'silentness' insisted on here is repeated from *The Ancient Mariner*, but here is an education that does not rely on guilt as it does there. Taught by a God whose vocabulary is nature, the child will enjoy a staff–student ratio as privileged as the one Wordsworth records in the early books of *The Prelude*. The child, who is not named in the poem and is known only by its 'gentle breathings', is Coleridge's son Hartley, named after the associationist philosopher David Hartley and given an associationist syllabus.

In a notebook entry of a few years later the obviousness and the general applicability of the associationist account is qualified. The insight comes this time from observation of the child Hartley rather than projection onto him as in the poem. The note ponders the origins of a sense of 'duty'. Duty may be associated with the commands or precepts of an authority figure and therefore with an interruption of childish 'pleasure', but this may not be an association that's generally made at all. It may rather have a more private significance. The phenomenon may be seen as symptomatic of a 'defect' shared by father and son: '*they most* labour under this defect who are most reverie-ish & streamy – Hartley, for instance & myself' (*CN* i. 1833). Being 'reverie-ish and streamy' may also be what characterizes the Ancient Mariner, but only at the cost of his punishment. The implication is that consciousness must be accompanied by conscience, the imagination by its own vigilant teacher. The child can guard against the 'lethargy of custom' (*BL* ii. 7), to which, as Coleridge writes later, the truths of religion even if accepted as such may fall prey among those who have not developed their Reason (*AR* 237). Hence 'by giving make it ask'.

The associationist education proposed in 'Frost at Midnight' is based not on the precepts of an actual school system but on the teaching of a God immanent in nature. In the poem the 'Great Universal Teacher' takes the place of the 'stern preceptor' of the poet's childhood. The latter is probably the more recognizable figure. Twenty years later Coleridge writes that, when conceived of as inculcating and acquiring knowledge, education fails to follow 'the method dictated by nature herself . . . the simple truth, that as all the forms in all organized existence, so must all true and living knowledge proceed from within, that it may be trained, supported, fed, excited, but can never be infused or impressed' (*F.* i. 500). Nature itself can be left to educate people in 'the objects of the senses'. What the child learns in the poem is as vague as what is learned by the Wedding Guest, but that is partly because the means of learning are more important than or take the place of the thing learned.

Coleridge goes on in the essay I have just quoted (the sixth of the *Essays on Method* in the 1818 *Friend*) to develop an analogy of world history with the process of human life. The world's childhood was the civilization of the Jews, characterized for Coleridge by faith and by the ability to bend 'objects of nature' to their purposes. The ancient Greeks carried humane, imaginative arts to 'ideal perfection' but were impractical. The Romans appropriated their achievements, placing them within a framework of 'war, empire, law!' (*F.* i. 505). The final stage, synthesizing the earlier ones and returning to the first, is Christianity. It is also implicitly synonymous with the attainment of 'a scientific method' in human growth, just as 'faith' and 'reason' were not opposed to each other but were united among the Jews. We will return in the next chapter to this account of history, but what is important here is that Christianity can provide a 'national education'. The analogy of history with the birth, growth, and decay of the human being depends on an organic view of the child and the state of childhood like that we saw in 'Frost at Midnight'.

In the poems written at the time of his closest relationship with the Wordsworths, and in the preface to *Lyrical Ballads* ('half the child of my own brain', as Coleridge claimed, let's remember), childhood and the novelty of its capacities as they appear to the adult are seen as ideal. This familiar idealization is made possible by speaking for the child rather than allowing it to speak for itself. The child is useful because of what it can do for *us*. The child is innocent and can restore the lost innocence of the adult. For Coleridge childhood is valuable not because it is a state of nature – that is, of absence – but because it is a state of imagination. He characterizes genius as the ability 'to carry on the feelings of childhood into the powers of manhood, to combine the child's sense of wonder and novelty with the appearances which every day for perhaps forty years had rendered familiar' (*F.* i. 109–10).

Newly liberal conceptions of the child in the late eighteenth century derive from both Locke and Rousseau: for the former, the child is plastic, moulded by experience – or, in an influential metaphor, 'white paper' – and could be 'fashioned as one pleases'; for the latter he or she is organic, having capacities for growth that civilization either fosters or distorts, and education is therefore analogous to cultivation. Advocates of a rational (or 'experimental') system of education and their 'Romantic' critics agreed on a more consensual, less coercive pedagogy and both stressed development and the acquisition of skills over rote-learning. Matters were different for poor children, whose education Alan Richardson describes as dominated by a 'project of "civilizing" the English poor (through a sort of internalized colonialism)'.[1] For Richardson, in revolutionary France and in Britain after Locke and Rousseau 'childhood' became politicized and the school displaced the Church as the primary apparatus of ideology. Education was one among several practices designed to ensure a harmoniously hierarchical state which depended on keeping its children innocent and on 'infantilizing' women and colonial subjects in order to do so. Women were 'infantilized at the same time as their role as educators of children and socializers of men [was] celebrated'.[2] Working-class education was partly self-education. Middle-class intellectuals and philanthropists recommended heuristic learning methods only in so far as they stopped short of questioning the hierarchy down which learning had formerly descended. An educated and dissatisfied working class threatened to replace savagery with monstrosity. Though these social practices are not homologous, children were misunderstood, and women, a newly self-conscious working class, and colonial subjects were 'infantilized' along with them: Frankenstein's monster, for instance, can be read as standing for any of all or these groups.

I want to qualify Richardson's account, but it does suggest reasons for Coleridge's interest in education. The 1809 Prospectus of *The Friend* promises that among the subjects of its essays will be 'Education in its widest sense, private, and national' (*F.* ii. 18). In the second number (June 1809) the general signs of moral improvement in society Coleridge lists include an interest in education (*F.* ii. 29–30), and if an account of the educational views of Sir Alexander Ball, the British High Commissioner in Malta to whom Coleridge had been private secretary, is a digression, then 'the increasing interest which men of all denominations feel in the bringing about of a national education, must be my excuse' (*F.* i. 541).

In practice, however, education might impede rather than foster 'the child's sense of wonder and novelty'. It was further from the ideal education posited at the end of 'Frost at Midnight' than to the schoolroom Coleridge remembers earlier in that poem as, in Wordsworth's famous lines from the 'Immortality Ode', 'Shades of the prison-house begin to close | Upon the growing boy'. This is why Coleridge was attracted to educational schemes which, in stressing the learner rather than the thing learned, seemed to accord with his own organic and dynamic principles.

Robert Southey's *A New System of Education* (1813), expanded from his articles in the *Quarterly Review* two years earlier, gives an account of the 'Madras' system of Dr Andrew Bell and Joseph Lancaster – so-called because Bell had experimented with it in an 'asylum' at Egmore near Madras for 'half-caste' sons of British soldiers in India. The system was based on using prefects or 'monitors' as teachers in a system of 'mutual improvement'. 'Self-tuition', Southey wrote, 'is the key-stone of the arch, – the main-spring of the watch, – the moving power of the whole machine.' So the Madras system is also known as the monitorial system. Similar experiments were then tried by Joseph Lancaster among the poor in Southwark. Coleridge was attracted to the systems of Bell and Lancaster for their domestic social utility, taking people off the parish and attending to their moral and religious education with a syllabus based chiefly on the Bible and the Anglican catechism. Lancaster's system was exported to Asia, Africa, and the West Indies, so education also performed a crucial imperial role, as is implicit, I think, in a comment made around this time which we will consider in a moment.

Southey's book was partly an intervention in the controversy between supporters of Bell and Lancaster as to who had actually originated the scheme, but more was at stake than the system's paternity. Adherents of the two men differed in how they regarded disobedience or misbehaviour. For Bell especially, stupidity or malevolence was a result of the way people had been treated in the past. This is a notion that has wider political implications – a notion that is crucial in Mary Shelley's *Frankenstein* and in her husband's poetry and prose, for instance, and in the latter it is explicitly used as a defence for the bloody excesses of the French Revolution. In Lancaster's schools, however, discipline was primary and was enforced by informing or surveillance. Punishment stressed public humiliation rather than pain; it was based on public contrition and demotion.

By the time Coleridge gave a lecture on education at the Royal Institution in May 1808 – which survives only in the notes of one who attended – he had come to believe that the monitorial system's emphasis on clock time, orderly behaviour, and decency was too crudely mechanistic. According to Southey, Coleridge announced of Lancaster's practice of punishment by humiliation, 'No boy who has been subject to punishments like these will stand in fear of Newgate, or feel any horror at the thought of a slave ship!' (*CN* iii. 3291 n.). Lancaster, a Quaker, had written that the school 'should be established on general christian principles, and on them only', and Coleridge also attacks Lancaster's advocacy of non-denominational religious education, rather than Anglican.

Thomas Clarkson the anti-slaver was among the audience for the lecture in which (or in a passage from *The Friend* which seems to derive from it), Coleridge called him, along with Bell, the two contemporaries 'who had done most for humanity':

> Were but a hundred men to combine a deep conviction that virtuous habits may be formed by the very means by which knowledge is communicated, that men may be made better, not only in consequence but *by* the mode and *in* the process, of instruction:

> were but an hundred men to combine that clear conviction of this, which I myself at this moment feel, even as I feel the certainty of my being, with a perseverance of a CLARKSON or a BELL, the promises of ancient prophecy would disclose themselves to our faith, even as when a noble castle hidden from us by an intervening mist, discovers itself by its reflection in the tranquil lake, on the opposite shore of which we stand gazing. (*F.* i. 103)

What is most striking here is the final image. The reflection of a phenomenon that cannot itself be seen gradually becomes visible. The process also recapitulates the ideal visualization of 'This Lime-tree Bower my Prison' in the way that it is through 'gazing' that 'thought' becomes material. So the image here is perhaps an image for faith as the ground of action or as making a difference which cannot be measured in utilitarian terms. High claims then are made here for education. It might lead us to the fulfilment of Biblical prophecy, confirming 'our faith'. The 'hundred men' who might initiate such a programme are given a name (though not actually numbered) in *Church and State*, as we shall see. In this passage education is seen to be valuable as process rather than product, for what it does rather than for what it makes. Education should not be instruction; rather it should be for '*educing* the faculties, and forming the habits' (*LS* 40).

Coleridge points, as he often does, to etymology to make the point, insisting that education *educe*: the learner is to be an educt rather than product; that is, to be led forth, elicited, or developed into something rather than to be made into something. This is not to be the libertarian enterprise it may sound but requires subordination, as is clear from a note in which Coleridge glosses ' educing' as 'eliciting the faculties of the human mind, and at the same time subordinating them to the reason and conscience, varying the means of this common end according to the sphere and the particular mode, in which the individual is likely to act and become useful' (*F.* i. 540*). Now that education was becoming mass education there were alarming implications for Coleridge. Wordsworth writes in a famous fragment that 'The Child is Father to the Man' but for Coleridge, now that 'Books are in every hovel', there is a new danger for the traditionally educated classes in that the child may read what will make him or her ungovernable as an adult: 'the Cottager's child sheds his first bitter tears over pages, which render it impossible for the man to be treated or governed as a child' (*LS* 39–40). Reading is too important to be left wholly to the reader, or learning to the learner. This last passage implies that enforcing on the working classes a state of infantilism is a good and desirable object, but it first appears in the sixth number of *The Friend* in September 1809 at the end of a more equivocal paragraph. Coleridge is characteristically sceptical about his age's self-description as enlightened. Nevertheless he is optimistic about the increasing capacity throughout Europe for 'reflection'. Such a capacity implies that even Bonaparte's gains are reversible (*F.* ii. 86). The Fall only occurs once and the knowledge that is its penalty is an equivocal penalty. Just as the Mariner's 'strange power of speech' may be a blessing as well as a curse, there are gains from this increase in thinking. In other words, we should be wary of assuming that the ideological function of education is merely to produce compliant subjects of the state, and wary of taking Coleridge to be an apologist for such a process. Advocacy of individual freedom (such as the child's freedom from authoritarian teaching) is not at all at odds with dismay at the uses to which that freedom may be put. There was a 1960s cartoon in which a grizzled war veteran watching some long-haired teenagers says 'we gave them freedom and then they go and do just what they like'. This apparent paradox is common in the Liberal tradition to which I argue Coleridge belongs.

Thus there is in *The Friend* a familiar colonialist argument offered regarding education, in a long paraphrase of what was purportedly the opinion of Sir Alexander Ball:

> no body of men can for any length of time be safely treated otherwise than as rational beings; and . . . therefore, the education of the lower classes was of the utmost consequence to the permanent security of the empire, even for the sake of our navy. The dangers, apprehended from the education of the lower classes, arose . . . entirely from its not being universal, and from the unusualness in the lowest classes of *those* accomplishments, which He, like Doctor Bell, regarded as one of the *means* of education, and not as education itself. If . . . the lower classes in general possessed but one eye or one arm, the few who were so fortunate as to possess two, would naturally become vain and restless, and consider themselves as entitled to a higher situation. He illustrated this by the faults attributed to learned women, and that the same objections were formerly made to educating women at all; namely, that their

> knowledge made them vain, affected, and neglectful of their proper duties. Now that all women of condition are well-educated, we hear no more of these apprehensions, or observe any instances to justify them. Yet if a lady understood the Greek one-tenth part as well as the whole circle of her acquaintances understood the French language, it would not surprise us to find her less pleasing from the consciousness of her superiority in the possession of an unusual advantage. (*F.* i. 540)

There is in this approving paraphrase what I have called a colonialist argument. Some are to be denied full rights within a state because they are poorly educated, but on the other hand to educate them may be to foster envy. Women are enrolled in this circular argument in the reactionary fastidiousness of the observation that female education will disturb manners. The first education must therefore be moral; that is, in those accomplishments, rare in the lower class, which are 'the means of education'. In *The Statesman's Manual* Coleridge says that the Madras system of education – which by this time he calls mere 'instruction' – may give its beneficiaries socially divisive aspirations, turning them into unruly subjects and thus 'become confluent with the evils it was intended to preclude' (*LS* 42). If the newly educated are not to get ideas above their station there is a need for them to be directed by what he will call the clerisy.

That term is coined in *On the Constitution of the Church and State*, but the role is described much earlier – it is what Coleridge sketches in the notebook entry on the 'public' discussed at the end of the previous chapter, and it also seems to be there in embryo in 'Religious Musings', written, according to the subtitle, on Christmas Eve 1794 (but actually not finished until 1796). In that poem Coleridge posits that 'the wretched Many' will be led out of their misery or even redeemed by 'eloquent men' who

> stung to rage by Pity,
> Have rous'd with pealing voice the unnumbered tribes
> That toil and groan and bleed, hungry and blind –
> These, hush'd awhile with patient eye serene,
> Shall watch the mad careering of the storm;
> Then o'er the wild and wavy chaos rush
> And tame the outrageous mass, with plastic might
> Moulding Confusion to such perfect forms,

As erst were wont...
To float before them...

(ll. 253–62)

There is an ideal here of Christ the teacher but also of radicals like Joseph Priestley, who later in the poem is called a saint and is enrolled in a pantheon also including Milton, Newton, and Hartley of those who could lead people out of bondage and calm the confusion. Later, in *Biographia Literaria*, the clergyman offers a secret ministry, 'the unobtrusive, continuous agency of a protestant church establishment' (*BL* i. 227) within his parish. Still later, the role of the clergy will be more widely assigned to a 'clerisy'. Coleridge's later positions may be incipient in the fraught optimism of the early 1790s. His own protests of consistency to 'principles' rest on finding later positions incipient in earlier ones in this kind of way. His later conservatism, however, changes the relative valuations of such an élite and 'many'. The élite come to be seen not as saviours of the many but as their priests; and the many, rather than being dangerous only because 'wretched', will come to be seen as tyrannous in themselves. In 1796, however, 'the wretched Many' are the victims of wrong and not its source.

In *The Friend* Coleridge adjures statesmen to know

> that a learned class is an essential element of a state – at least of a Christian state. But *you* wish for general illumination! You begin with the attempt to *popularize* learning and philosophy; but you will end in the *plebification* of knowledge. A true philosophy in the learned class is essential to a true religious feeling in all classes. (*F.* i. 447)

In the last work published in his lifetime, *On the Constitution of the Church and State* (1829), Coleridge represents education as the fundamental means of achieving numerous participating members of a state. He writes that such an aim will be achieved by means of what he calls a clerisy. This is an institution which, as was suggested by the notebook entry quoted at the end of the previous chapter, is to be supported by the state, though independent of it. It is to be supported by the 'nationalty' – property which is neither private nor held in trust for the nation by landowners but is set aside for the nation.

The purpose of the clerisy is to 'diffuse' what people need to know. Diffusing knowledge rather than instruction, the clerisy will replace the self-education of the newly literate classes. It is posed as counter to an ungoverned readership and a proliferation of publications:

> a permanent, nationalized, learned order, a national clerisy or church, is an essential element of a rightly constituted nation, without which it wants the best security alike for its permanence and its progression; and for which neither tract societies nor conventicles, nor Lancasterian schools, nor mechanics' institutions, nor lecture-bazaars under the absurd name of universities, nor all these collectively, can be a substitute. (*C&S* 69)

The clerisy is a body that will include teachers as well as clerics and indeed is mostly secular, but is left deliberately vaguely defined. The term originally referred, Coleridge says, to those who were learned 'in all the liberal arts and sciences' and not only theology, which was however primary

> because the SCIENCE of Theology was the root and trunk of the knowledge that civilized man, because it gave unity and the circulating sap of life to all other sciences, by virtue of which alone they could be contemplated as forming, collectively, the living tree of knowledge. It had the precedency, because under the name theology, were comprised all the main aids, instruments, and materials of NATIONAL EDUCATION, the *nisus formativus* of the body politic, the shaping and informing spirit, which *educing*, i.e. eliciting, the latent *man* in all the natives of the soil, *trains them up* to citizens of the country, free subjects of the realm. (*C&S* 48)

The insistence on the organic conceit here is revealing. 'Theology' is a tree synonymous with 'national education', all other disciplines being merely branches which it unifies and contains. Education in its turn again consists of what teaches or guides the learner to truth rather than of what he or she is instructed to do. Education is thus concerned with training 'free subjects' rather than producing compliant ones. We have seen though how ambiguous a process of 'educing' may be. The phrase *nisus formativus* here, quoted from the German anatomist Blumenbach, whose lectures Coleridge had attended at Göttingen, is translated by the editor of *Church and State* as 'formative urge, impulse, or force'. All things tend towards their final organic form, containing this tendency within themselves.

In the *Essays on Method* from the 1818 *Friend* 'method' is something like the 'reason' of Rousseau (though Coleridge loathed Rousseau): it is a capacity to posit ends and consequences which is not innate though the capacity for it is and which must therefore be learned. The development of method is like the development of the human being. There is a period when the child accumulates without learning, a period in which language is learned, then a period of potential during which the child can learn to use that language when it becomes vital that it is not impressed with outward or 'sensual' experience so that it may learn 'method' as the means of connecting with its purpose (*F.* i. 499–500). In the third of his course of lectures on the history of philosophy given in 1818–19 Coleridge praises Pythagoras for having contended 'that moral acts form an object of contemplation equally with all other acts' and determining this as a law which however could only be taught by example: 'he rested the whole chance of bringing men into a moral state upon education, and on this ground: that virtue, so far from being learned by any theory, could only be known by the practice of virtue; that there was no power of educing virtue out of anything else but itself; nay, more, that there was that which is supposed in all virtue, namely an act of the will'.[3]

In an earlier essay from *The Friend* Coleridge uses Francis Bacon as the authority for his imperative of Reason and the Idea, freed from the delusions of the understanding: 'that is, freed from the limits, the passions, the prejudices, the peculiar habits of the human understanding, natural or acquired; but above all, pure from the arrogance, which leads man to take the forms and mechanism of his own mere reflective faculty, as the measure of nature and of Deity' (*F.* i. 490). Only thus equipped, stripped for action, 'can the sciences attain to their full evolution, as the organs of one vital and harmonious body, [and] that most weighty and concerning of all sciences, the science of EDUCATION, be understood in its first elements, [and go on to] display its powers, as the nisus formativus of social man, as the appointed PROTOPLAST of true humanity' (*F.* i. 493). (Protoplast is a substance with vital properties, containing the secret of life. Coleridge then goes on to draw a distinction between civilization and cultivation also made in *Church and State*.)

An alternative translation of the phrase *nisus formativus* might be 'shaping power'. In the passage from *Church and State* quoted on page 39 the phrase is followed by the term 'shaping spirit' which recapitulates Coleridge's own famous term from his poem 'Dejection', 'my shaping spirit of Imagination'. Like the cleric, the poet 'diffuses' (*BL* ii. 16). In other words, theology and state theory already live pretty close to the aesthetic. What is said of the formative importance of education to the state suggests something of the importance of Coleridge's concept of the imagination.

The first volume of Coleridge's *Biographia Literaria* is largely concerned with an account of how he freed himself from the snares of the instrumental reason of Locke and Priestley there called 'understanding'. In *Church and State* Coleridge sees nineteenth-century Britain as increasingly ensnared by such utilitarian assumptions, caught in a long process of degeneration from the Elizabethan and Commonwealth periods he so admired.

In the thirteenth chapter of *Biographia Literaria* Coleridge 'condenses' his main thesis into two famous and baffling paragraphs which initially distinguish 'primary' and 'secondary' imagination:

> The IMAGINATION . . . I consider either as primary, or as secondary. The primary IMAGINATION I hold to be the living Power and prime Agent of all human Perception, and as a repetition in the finite mind of the eternal act of creation in the infinite I AM. The secondary I consider as an echo of the former, co-existing with the conscious will, yet still as identical with the primary in the *kind* of its agency, and differing only in *degree*, and in the mode of its operation. It dissolves, diffuses, dissipates, in order to re-create; or where this process is rendered impossible, yet still at all events it struggles to idealize and to unify. It is essentially *vital*, even as all objects . . . are essentially fixed and dead.
>
> FANCY, on the contrary, has no other counters to play with, but fixities and definites. The Fancy is indeed no other than a mode of Memory emancipated from the order of time and space; and blended with, and modified by that empirical phenomenon of the will, which we express by the word CHOICE. But equally with the ordinary memory it must receive all its materials ready made from the law of association. (*BL* i. 304–5)

Like the qualifying revisions of and the explanatory apparatus added to *The Ancient Mariner* and like the apologetic preface to the published version of 'Kubla Khan', this passage advertised as crucial comes hedged about by prior qualification. The climactic definition of imagination is preceded by 'A Chapter of requests and premonitions concerning the perusal or omission of the chapter that follows' and by a 'letter from a friend' which, though speaking in sublime terms of the reversal of the familiar and expected he or she experienced in reading the chapter which does not follow, finds that 'from the necessity of compression . . . what remains, looks . . . like the fragments of an old ruined tower' (*BL* i. 302–3). The letter persuades Coleridge to reserve the hundred pages or so the chapter occupies for his *Logosophia* or *Opus Maximum*, which did not appear in his lifetime. The author of the letter was, of course, Coleridge himself. Like the famous 'person . . . from Porlock' who interrupted the transcription of at least two or three hundred lines of 'Kubla Khan', the fictional correspondent was a necessary fiction.

The distinction of imagination from fancy in the second half of this passage joins a long eighteenth-century debate over the terms; it is the identification of a 'primary' and 'secondary' imagination which is new. This description, though, indicates some of the difficulties with the definition. To separate and to identify are opposites: which is Coleridge claiming to do for his doubled imagination? And are 'primary' and 'secondary' temporal or qualitative terms? What is clear is the pre-eminence of imagination in 'all human Perception'. For Coleridge the God who spoke the words 'I AM' to Moses is both the first principle of the universe and an absolute self-consciousness. If the 'primary imagination' is the element of this God-like quality in 'all' human beings, the 'secondary imagination' refers to the manner in which that self-consciousness is re-created, as art perhaps. If the primary imagination is intuitive, the secondary is analytic. When in this passage Coleridge collects a list of oppositions around the two terms imagination and fancy, the secondary imagination, he asserts, 'dissolves, diffuses, dissipates, in order to re-create' with an ultimate purpose to 'idealize and to unify'. It is a 'vital' principle capable of transforming an object-world which is 'essentially fixed and dead', elements of a material universe which the fancy is confined to shuffling around. Significantly, there is a temporal as well as a spatial dimension to the distinction, at least by analogy. Coleridge associates the 'fancy' with 'memory' and, by implication, the 'imagination' is a useful and progressive faculty of the present and future.

Imagination is 'that reconciling and mediatory power, which incorporating the Reason in Images of the Sense and organizing (as it were) the flux of the Senses by the permanence and self-circling images of the Reason, gives birth to a system of symbols, harmonious in themselves, and consubstantial with the truths, of which they are the *conductors*' (*LS* 28–9). Imagination 'incorporates' Reason, that is, it gives bodily or sensory form (as 'symbols') to what could not otherwise be apprehended by the bodily senses. Imagination ought to do in the aesthetic realm what Reason does in the realm of speculation, but it keeps leaking out, and over. At the end of the fullest account of his own aesthetics, in the last paragraph of *Biographia Literaria,* Coleridge reasserts the opposition of human and divine, and goes on:

> this alone can be my Defence . . . not without the consciousness of having earnestly endeavoured to kindle young minds and to guard them against the temptations of Scorners by showing that the Scheme of Christianity, as taught in the Liturgy and Homilies of our Church, though not discoverable by human reason, is yet in accordance with it; that link follows link by necessary consequence; that religion passes out of the ken of Reason only where the eye of Reason has reached its own Horizon; and that Faith is then but its continuation: even as the Day softens away into the sweet Twilight, and Twilight, hushed and breathless, steals into the Darkness. (*BL* ii. 247)

The passage invokes an 'unquenched desire' for a twilight state of transition from the aesthetic to the spiritual. The godlike quality in human beings which imagination approaches is the Reason. On the flyleaf of a copy of volume ii of *The Friend* Coleridge wrote 'It is wonderful, how closely Reason and Imagination are connected, and Religion the union of the two' (*F.* i. 203 n.). Understanding, 'the faculty by which we generalize and arrange the phaenomena of perception', is bound to the sensuous and temporal world of experience. The technological advances of Coleridge's lifetime may have made his age the apogee of understanding, he says, but there has been no parallel growth of Reason. 'Reason cannot exist without Understanding'(*F.* i. 156), but the understanding and experience can exist without Reason, as the world around him demonstrated. The state or culture must incorporate the truths of Reason just as the child must.

3

Church

Coleridge did find posthumously an attentive audience among Anglican thinkers: theirs were the 'young minds' he 'kindled'. John Sterling wrote in a letter of 1836: 'To Coleridge I owe *education*' (*AR*, p. cxiv). It is perhaps surprising that the passage from the *Biographia Literaria* quoted at the end of the previous chapter should assert that the truths of Reason accord with the rituals of the Church. We saw from *The Ancient Mariner* at the start that the ideal of the community was stronger than that of the kirk and Coleridge's movement from the Unitarianism of 'Religious Musings' to the high Anglicanism of his last years seemed to some to be of a piece with a movement from early radicalism to High Toryism.

In a pair of important essays published in 1838 and 1840, Mill called Coleridge with Jeremy Bentham 'the two seminal minds of the nineteenth century', not in terms of the direct influence of either but as 'the teachers of the teachers'. Platonic and Kantian terms such as 'Reason' and 'Idea' are in Coleridge always explicitly Christian too, and his influence on immediately succeeding generations was primarily as a teacher of Churchmen. Coleridge was teacher of the whole of the liberal Anglican school of John Sterling, Julius Hare, Connop Thirlwall, and Frederick Denison Maurice. In the dedication to his *Kingdom of Christ* (1842) Maurice salutes Coleridge for applying to theology the principle of Reason independent of experience which had succeeded 'the atheism of Hume' in the previous century:

> Nearly every thoughtful writer of the day would have taught us, that the highest truths are those which lie beyond the limits of Experience, that the essential principles of the Reason are those which cannot be proved by syllogisms, that the evidence for them is the impossibility of admitting that which does fall under the laws of

> experience, unless we recognize them as its foundation; nay the impossibility of believing that we ourselves are, or that anything is, except upon these terms.[1]

A secular writer, Walter Pater, saw the same things but valued them almost oppositely: Coleridge affirmed an 'absolute spirit' that was dying out in the nineteenth century to be replaced by an ethos of relativism, and this made him both heroic and comic. 'The literary life of Coleridge was a disinterested struggle against the application of the relative spirit to moral and religious questions,' Pater wrote in an essay published in 1866. 'Everywhere he is restlessly scheming to apprehend the absolute; to affirm it effectively; to get it acknowledged. Coleridge failed in that attempt, happily even for him, for it was a struggle against the increasing life of the mind itself.' His rearguard action is doomed to failure because 'all is fictitious from the beginning'.[2]

F. D. Maurice admires *The Ancient Mariner* and *Christabel* but 'question[s] whether I should be as interested as I am, even in these, if I did not discover in them many veins and fibres which seem to me to connect them with his personal being; if they did not help me to read more clearly the history of his mind, and therein the history of our time'.[3] We saw how the temptation to see Coleridge as his own Ancient Mariner was irresistible to many in Coleridge's own lifetime, but in Maurice's remark there's a near-synonymy of 'Coleridge's mind' with 'our time'. In Maurice's version Coleridge does not seem the quixotic figure struggling against the current that Pater represents but rather the opposite. His writings are said to reveal a 'personal being' who is at the same time representative. 'I own that the books of Mr. Coleridge are mainly interesting to me as the biography of one who passed through the struggles of the age to which we are succeeding.'[4] Maurice would agree with Pater that it was Coleridge's habitual quest for the principle or idea behind phenomena which lay at the centre of his thinking.

Coleridge wanted to show that revealed religion, far from being incompatible with Reason, was rather its major source: he wanted, as Elinor Shaffer puts it, 'Christian theology under the penetrating probes of Enlightenment criticism'.[5] Shaffer is referring to the Higher Criticism of the Bible, by German scholars such as Eichorn and Lessing, whose study of the contexts of its authors (which, as she shows, Coleridge knew even before going to Germany in 1798–9), demonstrated that not all the Bible was literally true. Its authors might have been inspired to write but were not necessarily taking dictation. In the third letter of the work his nephew published under the title *Confessions of an Inquiring Spirit* Coleridge gives the analogy of a biography, in which we do not expect everything to have been dictated by its subject (*SW* 1131–2). (As Lessing said, the Bible contains but does not constitute the Christian religion. Christianity was not true because the prophets and apostles taught it; they taught it because it was true.) One implication of the new biblical scholarship was to complicate and undermine fundamentalist religion, partly by showing that the fundamentals might actually be different from what they had been taken to be. Another consequence of this is that the earliest parts of the Bible – the Pentateuch, or five books of Moses, for instance – might be closest to the divine origin. Similar arguments were being made about secular as well as biblical texts, for example in the investigation of 'primitive' writings by scholars such as Hugh Blair and Robert Lowth, and, as we saw in the previous chapter, the child too might be seen as being closer to its divine origin than the adult. This has consequences for how we read history, as we shall see.

We saw from his early poems Coleridge's insistence on the inadequacy of the mere senses. In the previous chapter we saw him castigate what he sees as the present over-attachment to the senses, a gratification of immediate desires: scientific and technological developments in the present show that 'understanding' has reached its apogee but the state has artificially separated out and devalued the aesthetic from its education system to its own detriment. Understanding has usurped the place of 'Reason', which for Coleridge distinguishes people from animals and identifies them with the God in whose image they are made. Reason is thus a higher faculty than understanding which animals too may possess. Reason is standing back from or standing outside of the things the mind considers in order to consider the mind itself, just as 'the best part of human language, properly so called, is derived from reflection on the acts of the mind itself' (*BL* ii. 54). This suggests that poetry is or ought to be reflexive, self-consciously in the mode of critique, and I have suggested that even the early poems can be read in this way.

In the late poem 'Constancy to an Ideal Object' the poet seems to be another version of the Ancient Mariner who, if deprived of the completion of relationship,

> were but a becalmèd bark,
> Whose Helmsman on an ocean waste and wide
> Sits mute and pale his mouldering helm beside.
>
> (ll. 22–4)

In a sense the 'ideal object' of the title is Sara Hutchinson, the poem a record of the desire for 'a home, an English home, and thee!' The poem seems also to recapitulate 'Kubla Khan'. The Khan brought into being an energetic and even potentially erotic landscape attended by distant threats and ready perhaps to imprison the unwary. 'Constancy to an Ideal Object' is structurally similar. The poem has a kind of coda or afterthought, as 'Kubla Khan' does. The first paragraph of the poem is addressed to a second person who, because she is absent, cannot be 'embodied' and remains a 'yearning Thought'. In the earlier poem the coda moves from the third to the first person, from 'In Xanadu did Kubla Khan' to 'a vision once I saw'. The movement in this poem is rather the reverse of that. The poem's second paragraph is a long comparison of the absent beloved with an 'image' that might only be the reflection made by the solitary lover:

> And art thou nothing? Such thou art, as when
> The woodman winding westward up the glen
> At wintry dawn, where o'er the sheep-track's maze
> The viewless snow-mist weaves a glist'ning haze,
> Sees full before him, gliding without tread,
> An image with a glory round its head;
> The enamoured rustic worships its fair hues,
> Nor knows he makes the shadow, he pursues!
>
> (ll. 25–32)

The grammatical shift which occurs from first to third person is important. There's an attempt in this poem to realize or objectify a 'vision' less substantial than in 'Kubla Khan'. Both the risk and the reward are distanced or dulled by custom, and, if this vision cannot imprison, nor can it embrace.

'The Brocken Spectre' referred to also in *Aids to Reflection* is, as

Richard Holmes explains in the notes to his selection of Coleridge's poetry, 'a rare atmospheric phenomenon produced by the sun's rays throwing the viewer's shadow horizontally forward on to low cloud or mist, and encircling it with a rainbow spectrum generated by refraction of the light through water droplets. It can occur on any mountain top, at dawn or dusk; and can also be observed from aircraft'.[6] Despite having climbed the Brocken during his stay in Germany, Coleridge had not actually seen this famous optical illusion. In 'Constancy to an Ideal Object' the aesthetic and the ethical are assimilated to each other again, but here they stand against what might be called the epistemological. The image may be beautiful as well as good but it may have no objective existence. This is only the embodiment of a thought which, though constant in a mutable world, may only be a projection or emanation of the beholder. There is no longer an ideal of reciprocity so much as a distrust of the sublime appearance. Hence the unanswerable question 'And art thou nothing?' (l. 25). Is the ideal inside or outside the poet? Is the poet to be equated not only with the unrequited lover of the first paragraph but also with 'the enamoured rustic' of the second, who is virtuous because he is constant and does his duty?

The questions arise because of the poet's distrust of common understanding, which we saw represented by his distrust of the reading public in Chapter 1. The constant narrator has reached no 'vantage-ground' and is still 'midway'. The implication of Coleridge's critique of Wordsworth is that poetry ought to begin with meditation rather than observation. However, the implication of this poem is that it might not be possible to discern actualization of the idea; that, in other words, re-entry to the world of understanding might not be possible. For the poet this would mean being left like the Ancient Mariner in a condition of exile. For the citizen it would mean inhabiting a disintegrated state.

Coleridge's idea of history too is derived from 'reflection on the acts of the mind itself'. History cleared of contingency would reveal itself to be providential. National histories must be the history of Christianity, he says in the first letter of *Confessions of an Inquiring Spirit*, and 'all History must be *Providential*' (*SW* 1119). We saw a compressed version of such a history in an essay from *The Friend* discussed in the previous chapter in which the ancient Jews were a nation faithful to Reason exemplified by a living God, and the Greeks represented a triumph of understanding in seeing such a pre-existent being as material. The synthesis of the two is to be in Christianity, coupling the revelation of the divine to the Reason within the human mind. This scheme is threaded through Coleridge's later writings and is given its fullest exposition in a lecture delivered to the Royal Society of Literature in 1825 'On the Prometheus of Aeschylus' in which Coleridge reads both the Greek tragedy and the myth on which it is based as concerned with the origin to human *nous* or reason, just as the Jewish sacred texts are. The maturity of a state as of an individual is apparent as a separation or specialization which ought to be the prelude to the higher unity of philosophy. 'In the Greek [civilization]', he writes, 'we see already the dawn of approaching manhood. The substance, the *stuff*, is philosophy, the *form* only is poetry' (*SW* 1267).

Such a conception of history informs Coleridge's analysis of the present too. In an 1826 letter to John Hookham Frere he wrote that the 'purpose' of history was 'to exhibit the moral necessity of the whole in the freedom of the component parts: the resulting chain necessary, each particular link remaining free' (*CL* vi. 583). Among actual historians, Gibbon and Hume were trivial chroniclers of cause and effect; only Herodotus and the writers of the Hebrew Bible showed the law of the whole with the freedom of the parts. *The Statesman's Manual* (1816) argues for the sufficiency of the bible for epochal as well as daily life: the Jewish sacred writings 'flow from principles and ideas that are not so properly said to be confirmed by reason as to be reason itself!' (*LS* 17). But this should not be confused with abstraction. In that work the biblical histories are said to be about people not things, not products of the understanding but '*educts* of the Imagination' (*LS* 29). Coleridge praises a similar coexistence of the individual and the universal in secular writings, such as those of Shakespeare, but it is mainly in the Scriptures that 'both Facts and Persons must of necessity have a twofold significance, a past and a future, a temporary and a perpetual, a particular and a universal application' (*LS* 30). One of the clerisy's functions too would be to 'bind the present with the past' (*C&S* 43).

A constitution then should bind together the tendencies to

permanence and to progression in a state; it should balance the contending powers. The word 'constitution' had for Coleridge the dynamic sense of a verbal noun. The 'English Constitution', he wrote in an 1804 notebook, 'arising gradually & according to no plan, out of the nature of things adapted itself to the moral nature of Things, Struggles between the King una cum populo, & the aristocracy between the People and the King &c &c,/ introduced checks and a spirit of suspicion suitable to the effects of Power on the human Character' (*CN* ii. 2076). This organic, balanced constitution stands in for a 'national interest' spuriously appealed to for instance by the French. In *On the Constitution of the Church and State* Coleridge can claim, as Edmund Burke had done, that an unwritten constitution is superior because it is an 'idea'. He promises to explain the constitution of Church and State 'according to the idea of each'.

An idea is separate from any manifestation of it and thus slides off into an ideal. The 'idea' is not visible to all because it underlies phenomena and institutions and is 'that conception of a thing... which is given by the knowledge of *its ultimate aim*' (*C&S* 12). An idea is neither sensuous nor an abstraction from the understanding but 'an educt of the Imagination actuated by the pure Reason' (*LS* 113–14) and as such it can be called 'that most glorious birth of the God-like within us' (*LS* 50). The idea is the internal or subjective version of what objectively or externally is law (*C&S* 13). But the idea of a state is teleological and may be independent of any state that had actually existed. The ideal Church is no less idealistically conceived than the community posited in 'Frost at Midnight' as a kind of congregation.

The national Church is distinct from the Christian Church and a state must be grasped as a totality, as an idea. If a state is independent of individuals, it is also independent of history: though states change, the idea of a state does not. A state founded on an 'idea' will be superior to and more permanent than one attempting to found itself on the short-term profit and loss of political economy. Coleridge found what he calls the 'mechano-corpuscular' philosophy of Locke and Hartley underlying the new science all the way to the economics of Malthus and Ricardo. In criticizing that tradition a quarter century after Coleridge's death, Marx famously wrote that changes in consciousness do not cause changes in material conditions, but are caused by them. Coleridge's view is diametrically opposite: 'the most important changes in the commercial relations of the world had their origin in the closets or lonely walks of uninterested theorists' (*LS* 14). As we have seen, commercial society ought for its own good to support such theorists.

Church and State claims to synthesize the ostensibly antithetical interests of landed and commercial society. They are opposites not contraries, which is to say that their interests can be reconciled (*C&S* 10). Within a state there are forces for permanence and progression. Permanence is represented by those of real (that is, landed) property for whom liberty is a privileged birthright, while progression is represented by those of mobile property (that is, the mercantile economy) whose knowledge and abilities make for 'an expanding liberty'. The *nouveau riche* merchant too will be altered when he purchases an estate, and 'redeems himself by becoming the staple ring of the chain, by which the present will become connected with the past; and the test and evidency of permanency afforded' (*C&S* 25). So land restrains a commercial sector which in its turn brings material progress, refinement, sociability, and the energy of emulation. The idea is one of a balance of permanence and progression in the state, coupled with a balance of national with Christian interests in the Church. A national Church, like a national education, will be one fitted not just to a supposed national character but to Britain's role as the most commercially successful state and the most powerful maritime empire to have existed. Coleridge's equivocation is such that the balance of powers in the contemporary, unreformed constitution of Britain implicitly realizes this idea.

A balance of apparently competing interests in a state is the ideal of a great deal of Enlightenment political theory, and an ideal which, where the theorist is British, is usually found to be realized in Britain. Coleridge adds to it a temporal dimension in which the present is to be balanced with the past. In the constitutional arguments of the 1790s both radicals and conservatives appealed to a constitution established by Magna Carta or at the Glorious Revolution of 1688 or to a 'primitive' past. Rather than the English constitution alone, Coleridge appeals in *Church and State* to the model of the ancient Jewish commonwealth and elsewhere envisages in the present (or near-future) its synthesis with the Greek roots of the West in a Christian civilization. This understanding of history is an ambitious set of terms for seeing present politics, but it may only be mystifying; certainly it could do nothing for attempts at constitutional reform. In *The Statesman's Manual* he urges on the upper classes a historical and typological reflectiveness as the best means of addressing circumstances still similar to those Wordsworth had identified in the preface to the *Lyrical Ballads*:

> If there be any antidote to that restless craving for the wonders of the day, which in conjunction with the appetite for publicity is spreading like an efflorescence on our national character; if there exist means for deriving resignation from general discontent, means of building up with the very materials of political gloom that stedfast frame of hope which affords the only certain shelter from the throng of self-realizing alarms, at the same time that it is the natural home and workshop of all the active virtues; that antidote and these means must be sought for in the collation of the present with the past, in the habit of thoughtfully assimilating the events of our own age to those of the time before us. (*LS* 8–9)

The historical 'assimilation' proposed here might have been given a model in *Church and State*. The ideal balance posited there between permanence and progression is carried over from aesthetic speculation in which imagination is recognized by a 'balance or reconciliation of opposite or discordant qualities' (*BL* ii. 16).

Mill, reviewing the second edition of *Church and State*, said that Coleridge asked of every institution not 'is it true?' but 'what is the meaning of it?'. The 'idea' or 'ultimate aim' of the state, Coleridge asserts, is distinct from the utilitarian aims he then saw gaining ground (in education for instance), aims which are short term, temporary, belonging to the understanding rather than the reason. This is the basis of a distinction between civilization and cultivation he makes at the end of Chapter 4.

Coleridge offers then a metaphysics of the state in a self-consciously rearguard action which restates the problems of a commercial society in metaphysical and spiritual terms. (So moral reform needs to come before extension of the franchise.) For Mill, though, an act of salvage is possible, an act which could potentially override Coleridge's Toryism with the progressive aspects of Mill's own liberalism. So, in his last work Coleridge offered a classic conservative view of British institutions that is sometimes reactionary too. (In a late poem he puns on 'reform' as 'riff-raff-form', and the table talk is much more explicit in its opposition to reform.) However, *Church and State* is abstract enough to appeal to the opposite camp too. Mill is right to suggest that much of it could be recuperated for liberalism.

The occasion of *Church and State* was the Catholic Emancipation Bill of 1829, though, as the account of it in this chapter suggests, it was hardly an intervention in that controversy. Calling a work of art 'occasional' limits its applicability to its first context. It is, of course, a rough but characteristic test of aesthetic worth that a work should be autonomous of its occasions – indeed this is a test Coleridge recommends be applied, for instance, to Shakespeare. We began this book by sketching a reading of *The Ancient Mariner* in such terms, as an allegory separate from its occasion. We went on to use that poem as a way of introducing three kinds of community with which Coleridge's voluminous writings are concerned, audience, education, and Church. The model *Church and State* offers was too abstract to be imitated, too full stylistically of what it assimilated to be more than an esoteric classic. In Chapter 1 we saw Coleridge defend prolixity as a necessary consequence of any sympathetic investigation. His tendency to be prolix and his abstraction, rather than being stylistic tics or flaws, are necessary results of an enterprise I have described as Liberal. It is these characteristics of Coleridge's writing to which we shall turn first in the conclusion.

Conclusion

Coleridge died in 1834. This book has to stop short of discussing his nineteenth-century and subsequent influence but the question of influence is a fascinating one not least because it *is* a question: Carlyle, Maurice, and Mill, to list only some who were broadly sympathetic to Coleridge, are left with a paraphrase of the Wedding Guest's question: what then must we do? The question arises for two main reasons, both of them charges made against Coleridge in his lifetime. The first is the difficulty of his sentences. As Coleridge himself summarizes the charge in the *Biographia Literaria,* there is 'a disproportionate demand on the attention ... an excess of refinement in the mode of arriving at truths ... beating the grounds for that which might have been run down by the eye ... the length and laborious construction of my periods; in short ... obscurity and the love of paradox' (*BL* i. 220). The elaborateness of a prose in which often more than justice is done to the question Mill said Coleridge asked ('What is the meaning of it?') always threatens to turn its ideal of equipoise into equivocation. We saw from the previous chapter that the equivocation is a tendency of his thinking as well as a tic of his writing.

The second reason why Coleridge is difficult is related to the first: the tendency of his writing to generalization or abstraction. The questions are to be answered at a venue where Christianity is crossed with Kant, and Kant with Plato. This was not necessarily a negative tendency as far as Coleridge was concerned. Philosophy and religion join poetry, he notes, in causing 'tranquillity & the attachment of the affections to *generalizations*' (*CN* ii. 2194). But again Coleridge seems to anticipate the charge when he notes the existence of a '*thinking* disease' (exemplified by the Germans after Kant) in which abstraction performs in a closed circuit and 'in which feelings instead of embodying themselves in *acts*, ascend . . . & become materials of general reasoning & intellectual pride' (*CN* iii. 4012). For Coleridge we should not though confuse the pathology of a function with the function itself. Abstraction is a necessary stage in any process of thinking but it is not the final stage. Logic, he writes, 'is but a cabinet of many drawers and pigeonholes, all empty. But are we, therefore, to procure no cabinets, and content ourselves with lumber-rooms and slut-corners?' (*L.* 204), and, in so far as abstraction is a tendency worthy of blame, the charge does not apply to religion, of which the first of the great truths he lists in an earlier notebook entry mined for the 1818 *Friend* (*F.* i. 431–5) is 'that Religion has no *speculative* dogmas – but all practical – all appealing to the will, & therefore all imperative' (*CN* iii. 3581).

This is the language of Kantian ethics in which practice is the movement outward into the world of the understanding. But the characteristic equivocations show an attachment to the contingent and various even when there is an absolute imperative. So, as we have seen, even while the audience needed moulding into the 'fit audience though few' Milton envisaged for his epic, there is a recognition that contemporary prophets needed funding in order to do so. The audience becomes an idea which the state needs to actualize before the job is done by a forgetful and amoral market. Coleridge's struggle to educate his readers as a fit audience for his theories influenced the content of those theories so that it becomes difficult to abstract or paraphrase his thought from his writing and, for instance, to number him among the post-Kantian philosophers. For that reason this book has been structured around three areas of his recurrent concern, beginning with the audience which *The Ancient Mariner* makes dramatically central.

As we have seen, friends and family functioned as the putative first audiences within many of Coleridge's poems of the 1790s and the Wordsworths played the part of a surrogate family, bridging the gap between speech and writing. At the close of 'To William Wordsworth' the poet's voice is succeeded by a 'happy vision of belovèd faces' (l. 107). A similar confidence in an immediate community enabled the conversation of 'Frost at Midnight', a poem in which the circle is widened to include the cooperation of the divine – indeed a poem in which God speaks intelligibly. There Coleridge's language, like that of Edmund Burke, appeals to familial sentiment rather than to ideological interest. In the introductory address to *Conciones ad Populum* Coleridge counters William Godwin's assertion of the inevitability ('necessity') of progress towards general benevolence with a Burkean insistence on familial example: 'The paternal and filial duties discipline the Heart and prepare it for the love of all Mankind. The intensity of private attachments encourages, not prevents, universal Benevolence' (*L. 1795*, 46). Coleridge attempts to repeat or replicate a language of intimacy in the public domain and his politics might be seen as an attempt to replicate the sustenance of an intimate or familial discourse on a public level.

Whatever the kind of language used among members of a family, it is, of course, *spoken* language; but it cannot be representative speech in the sense in which Coleridge in an early lecture praises Thelwall as 'the voice of tens of thousands' (*L. 1795*, 297). The difference between public and private language may then be one of context rather than of content. There is a gap between the 'community' of friends or family, invocation of which is a common feature in the early poems, and the 'audience' of subsequent readers. Once 'self' and 'audience' come to be seen as empirical rather than essentialist terms, we have to see Coleridge participating in a competition of discourses. Readers of Coleridge have to learn to attend patiently to local utterances and the discursive constraints upon them.

For instance, Coleridge's debt in the 1790s to the radical etymologist Horne Tooke has provided important evidence for those who want to recuperate him as a consistent radical. Under the influence of Tooke, Coleridge could see in the native vernacular both a suppressed history and the possibility of progress, a repository of communal value older than the absolutism of the then Prime Minister, of the established Church or the monarchy. Later, as he moved closer to the positions of these institutions, Coleridge's protests of consistency may only as it were anticipate the retrospective unity to any author's career provided by his or her biography. If his poems attempt to make an intimate language do the work of achievement in the religious and social realms, loading that language, or even overloading it, it is easy to obtrude biographical upon linguistic event and to assume that the linguistic collapse that is threatened by this overload must therefore also be personal collapse.

Coleridge's apparently private and often cryptic notebook entries might be seen as occupying a space between the poems and the often difficult 'symbolic language' of the later prose. Like diary entries or 'private' letters, such notes of course have an ambiguous status that is not wholly private. The audience imagined even for his published writings was a coterie audience. In *The Friend* Coleridge refers ironically to 'our *enlightened* age' and asks whether 'the Jacob's ladder of Truth, let down from heaven . . . is now the common highway, on which we are content to toil upward to the objects of our desires' (*F.* i. 58–9). This is a rhetorical question the answer to which is no. Truth is nevertheless a spring which becomes a stream (*F.* i. 65). The 'diffusion' of reason and poetry will lead to social progress or at least to the arrest of nearly two centuries of decline. It might be possible to recuperate Coleridge's private (indeed esoteric and élitist) spirituality for the public sphere by claiming him as a prophet of cultural diversity rather than of the unity of the divine spirit immanent in an archaically hierarchical society.

Coleridge's eclectic raiding of discourses might be seen as pluralist, even democratic. This is to say that the Coleridge who could be recuperated for Liberalism is not incommensurate with the apologist for conservatism. Hazlitt's Coleridge need not be incommensurate with Mill's. In literary criticism, for instance, his influence is evident in the assumption of organic form and in the 'practical criticism' – a term Coleridge coins in *Biographia Literaria* (*BL* ii. 19) – dominant until recently in the academy; there is much less evidence for the influence of the speculative, philosophically fraught arguer in the margins of books. His own writings need to be seen neither as constituting a system in themselves nor as the elegiac fragments of one. Rather, their chief interest may lie in a set of writings which most resist propositional summary. Magnificent modern editions enable us to read unpublished and often fragmentary texts – marginalia, schemes for unfulfilled projects, lecture notes, and notebooks – in which Mill's version of the question and the Liberal ideal embodied in it continue to echo.

People are not likely to emancipate themselves after reading Coleridge (nor perhaps feel that this is a goal that is possible, or even desirable), as they demonstrably strove to after reading the prose of Tom Paine, Godwin, or Shelley, but his resistance to commodification and to the hiving-off and devaluation of the aesthetic make him exemplary still. In this book Coleridge has been read not as a Tory apologist but as a sort of élitist Liberal; his dissatisfactions with the present make him, sporadically, progressive as well as reactionary. He has been read as a thinker engaged in the sympathetic critique of systems, rather than as a builder of systems. He has been read, too, as someone who 'struggles', as he wrote of the secondary imagination, to 'idealize and to unify'; who struggles to make an audience a 'friend', to see poetry as a mode of thought, to revive the 'magnetic' link of Church and State. This was not an enterprise predestined to fail, as Pater thought, but it swam against the currents that have brought us to the present.

Notes

INTRODUCTION

1. See A. W. Brian Simpson, *Cannibalism and the Common Law: The Story of the Tragic Last Voyage of the* Mignonette *and the Strange Legal Proceedings to which it Gave Rise* (Chicago: University of Chicago Press, 1984).
2. This is the wording of the first of the specific treasons defined by a statute of Edward III under which Thelwall and the others were arraigned, as quoted by John Barrell in an important essay on the treason trials, 'Imaginary Treason, Imaginary Law: The State Trials of 1794', in *The Birth of Pandora and the Division of Knowledge* (London: Macmillan, 1992), 119–43, at 122.
3. Thomas Love Peacock, *Nightmare Abbey*, in *The Novels of Thomas Love Peacock* (1948; corrected edn., ed. David Garnett, 2 vols., London: Rupert Hart-Davis, 1963), i. 360.
4. Thomas Carlyle, 'Coleridge', part I, chapter viii of *The Life of John Sterling*, in *The Works of Thomas Carlyle* (Centenary Edition, 30 vols.; London: Chapman & Hall, 1897), xi. 54, 56, 57.
5. *The Complete Works of William Hazlitt*, ed. P. P. Howe (21 vols.; London: Dent, 1930–4), vii. 114–16.

CHAPTER 1. AUDIENCE

1. Caroline Fox, *Memories of Old Friends*, ed. Horace N. Pym (London: Smith Elder, 1881), 12.
2. 'Mr Coleridge', in *The Complete Works of William Hazlitt*, ed. P. P. Howe (21 vols.; London, 1930–4), xi. 28–38, at 30.
3. As the context for his own poem, Wordsworth remembers Thelwall on his visit to Coleridge.

   > He really was a man of extraordinary talent, an affectionate husband, and a good father. Though brought up in the city on a tailor's board, he was

truly sensible of the beauty of natural objects. I remember once when Coleridge, he, and I were seated together upon the turf on the brink of a stream in the most beautiful part of the most beautiful glen of Alfoxden, Coleridge exclaimed, 'This is a place to reconcile one to all the jarrings and conflicts of the wide world.' – 'Nay,' said Thelwall, 'to make one forget them altogether.' (Michael Mason (ed.), *Lyrical Ballads* (Longman Annotated Texts; London: Longman, 1992), 346–7.)

4. Anna Laetitia Barbauld, 'To Mr C[olerid]ge', in Andrew Ashfield (ed.), *Romantic Women Poets, 1770–1838: An Anthology* (Manchester: Manchester University Press, 1995), 21–2.

CHAPTER 2. EDUCATION

1. Alan Richardson, *Literature, Education, and Romanticism: Reading as Social Practice, 1780–1832* (Cambridge: Cambridge University Press, 1994), 83.
2. Richardson, *Literature, Education, and Romanticism*, 173.
3. *The Philosophical Lectures of Samuel Taylor Coleridge*, ed. Kathleen Coburn (London: Routledge & Kegan Paul, 1949), 118–19.

CHAPTER 3. CHURCH

1. F. D. Maurice, *The Kingdom of Christ; or, Hints to a Quaker* (2nd edn., London: Macmillan, 1842), p. xxv. The second edition contains (i, pp. v–xxii) a dedicatory letter to Derwent Coleridge with the eulogy quoted in this chapter.
2. Walter Pater, 'Coleridge's Writings', in *Essays on Literature and Art*, ed. Jennifer Uglow (London: Everyman, 1973), 3, 6.
3. Maurice, *Kingdom of Christ*, p. x.
4. Ibid., p. viii.
5. Elinor Shaffer, *'Kubla Khan' and the Fall of Jerusalem* (Cambridge: Cambridge University Press, 1975), 32.
6. *Samuel Taylor Coleridge: Selected Poetry*, ed. Richard Holmes (Penguin Poetry Library; Harmondsworth: Penguin, 1996), 325.

Select Bibliography

WORKS BY COLERIDGE

The Collected Works of Samuel Taylor Coleridge, general editors Kathleen Coburn and Bart Winer (Bollingen Series LXXV; London: Routledge and Princeton: Princeton University Press, 1969–). Volumes published so far are listed alphabetically below, followed by the volume number in the *Collected Coleridge* (*CC*).

Aids to Reflection, ed. John Beer (1993), *CC*, vol. ix.

Biographia Literaria, ed. James Engell and Walter Jackson Bate (2 vols.; 1983), *CC*, vol. vii.

Essays on his Times, ed. David V. Erdman (3 vols.; 1978), *CC*, vol. iii.

The Friend, ed. Barbara E. Rooke (2 vols.; 1969), *CC*, vol. iv.

Lay Sermons, ed. R. J. White (1972), *CC*, vol. vi.

Lectures 1795: On Politics and Religion, ed. Lewis Patton and Peter Mann (1971), *CC*, vol. i.

Lectures 1808–19: On Literature, ed. R. A. Foakes (2 vols.; 1987), *CC*, vol. v.

The Logic, ed. J. R. de J. Jackson (1981), *CC*, vol. xiii.

Marginalia, ed. George Whalley (5 vols., 3 published so far; 1984–), *CC*, vol. xii.

On the Constitution of the Church and State, ed. John Colmer (1976), *CC*, vol. x.

Opus Maximum, ed. Thomas MacFarland, *CC*, vol. xv.

Shorter Works and Fragments, ed. H. J. Jackson and J. R. de J. Jackson (2 vols.; 1995), *CC*, vol. xi.

Table Talk, ed. Carl Woodring (2 vols.; 1990), *CC*, vol. xiv.

The Watchman, ed. Lewis Patton (1970), *CC*, vol. ii.

Coleridge, E. H. (ed.), *Coleridge: Poetical Works*, (2 vols.; Oxford: Oxford University Press, 1912). J. C. C. Mays's edition of the poems for the Collected Coleridge is still forthcoming at the time of writing. In the meantime this has been the standard text, at least until the appearance of William Keach's edition for Penguin (see below).

John Beer, (ed.), *Coleridge: Poems*, (2nd edn., London: Dent, 1974). A scholarly and very usable edition.

Holmes, Richard (ed.), *Samuel Taylor Coleridge: Selected Poetry* (Penguin Poetry Library; Harmondsworth: Penguin, 1996). This is an attractive, usefully annotated edition, although some would quarrel with Holmes's decision to arrange the poems in categories designed to reveal an autobiographical narrative.

Keach, William (ed.), *Samuel Taylor Coleridge: The Complete Poems* (London: Penguin, 1997). This edition appeared while the present book was in proof. It follows the policy of the series to print the latest published texts of the poems, although it also lists variants and contains both the 1798 and the 1834 versions of *The Ancient Mariner*. The annotation is excellent.

Wallen, Martin (ed.), *Coleridge's* Ancient Mariner*: An Experimental Edition of Texts and Revisions 1798–1828* (New York: Station Hill Literary Editions, 1993).

BIOGRAPHY

Ashton, Rosemary, *The Life of Samuel Taylor Coleridge: A Critical Biography* (Oxford: Blackwell, 1996).

Holmes, Richard, *Coleridge: Early Visions* (London: Hodder & Stoughton, 1989). The first volume of two.

Lefebure, Molly, *Samuel Taylor Coleridge: A Bondage of Opium* (New York: Stein & Day, 1974).

Pite, Ralph (ed.), *Coleridge, Lives of the Great Romantics II: Keats, Coleridge and Scott*, general ed. John Mullan (3 vols.; London: Pickering & Chatto, 1996), vol ii. A full and very useful collection of extracts from nineteenth-century memoirs and biographies.

CRITICAL AND SCHOLARLY WORKS

Some of the best material in this section is to be found in the editors' introductions to individual volumes of the Bollingen *Collected Coleridge* listed above, but see also:

Beer, John, *Coleridge's Poetic Intelligence* (London: Macmillan, 1977).

Especially excellent in its account of Coleridge's early intellectual formation.

Edwards, Pamela J., 'Liberty and Continuity in the Political Thought of Samuel Taylor Coleridge, 1794–1834 (unpublished Ph.D. thesis, University College, London, 1995). A vigorous argument for the continuity of 'principles' and for Coleridge as Liberal.

Everest, Kelvin, *Coleridge's Secret Ministry: The Context of the Conversation Poems 1795–1798* (Hassocks, Sussex: Harvester Press, 1979).

Hamilton, Paul, *Coleridge's Poetics* (Oxford: Blackwell, 1983). A reading of *Biographia Literaria* is central to this important account of the continued radical or at least democratic potential of Coleridge's thinking about language, especially the language of poetry.

Harding, Anthony J., *Coleridge and the Inspired Word* (Kingston and Montreal: McGill/Queens University Press, 1985). A learned and subtle account of Coleridge's reading of the Bible, usefully supplementing Elinor Shaffer's book (see below), and of his influence on the Oxford Movement, Augustus, and J. C. Hare at Cambridge, and the Platonists around James Marsh at the University of Vermont.

Jackson, J. R. de J. (ed.), *Coleridge: The Critical Heritage* (London: Routledge & Kegan Paul, 1970); *Coleridge: The Critical Heritage, ii. 1834–1900* (London: Routledge, 1991).

Keane, Patrick J., *Coleridge's Submerged Politics*: The Ancient Mariner *and* Robinson Crusoe (Columbia: University of Missouri Press, 1994). A full and fascinating account of *The Ancient Mariner* (and incidentally of *Robinson Crusoe*) which reads the spectre-bark as a slave ship and the comparison of rigging to 'a dungeon grate' through which the sun peers (l. 171) as representing Pittite oppression. You are, however, advised to skip the two introductions unless you do not find the lengthy restatement of liberal credentials tedious.

Klancher, Jon, *The Making of English Reading Audiences 1790–1832* (Madison, Wis.: University of Wisconsin Press, 1987). A bold account of the growth of reading audiences in the 'Romantic' period and of the consequences for writers and readers, taking Coleridge as a representative if not exemplary figure.

Leask, Nigel, *The Politics of Imagination in Coleridge's Critical Thought* (London: Macmillan, 1988). Though difficult, this is probably the best account of Coleridge's whole career which patiently makes material his vocabulary of 'imagination', 'idea', and 'reason' and is particularly illuminating on the late theological writings.

MacFarland, Thomas, *Coleridge and the Pantheist Tradition* (Oxford: Clarendon Press, 1969). This book is still an impressive account of Coleridge's philosophical relation to Spinoza and those who followed him, and marshalls its scholarship lucidly, although its claims for the unity and coherence of Coleridge's own philosophical enterprise seem overstated.

Mill, John Stuart, 'Coleridge', in *Mill on Bentham and Coleridge*, ed. F. R. Leavis (London: Chatto & Windus, 1950; repr. Cambridge: Cambridge University Press, 1980).

Orsini, G. N. G., *Coleridge and German Idealism* (Carbondale, Ill.: S. Illinois University Press, 1969). With MacFarland's book (see above) this is still an indispensable scholarly treatment of Coleridge's debt (some say amounting to plagiarism) to Schelling, Fichte, and other post-Kantian philosophers.

Richardson, Alan, *Literature, Education and Romanticism: Reading as Social Practice, 1780–1832* (Cambridge: Cambridge University Press, 1994). Full of information about the arguments over education in the period, usefully revising assumptions that 'Romantic' preoccupations with childhood are necessarily more radical than those by conservatives and evangelicals, though perhaps too ready to see a homology of the infantilization of women and 'primitive' peoples with a primitivization of children.

Shaffer, Elinor, *'Kubla Khan' and the Fall of Jerusalem* (Cambridge: Cambridge University Press, 1975). A pioneering scholarly account of Coleridge's relations to the German 'Higher Criticism' and its presence in the plans for Coleridge's unwritten epic.

Stillinger, Jack, *Coleridge and Textual Instability: The Multiple Versions of the Major Poems* (New York: Oxford University Press, 1994). A salutary reminder that familiar poems have several versions and a convincing argument that we read the poems *as* versions.

Index